I0644288

Tales of the Tuatha Dé Danann

New Translations of Irish Myths

Volume 1

What People Are Saying About

Tales of the Tuatha De Danann, Volume 1

Anyone who loves Irish mythology should read these translations if only to get a sense of how different the original stories really are from most of the retellings. This book is especially important for anyone interested in Irish paganism or spirituality, as most translations leave out crucial passages, which are included and translated here. To me, these versions are all about getting closer to the source, getting closer to the authentic heart of ancient pagan Ireland.
Christopher Scott Thompson, author of *Pagan Anarchism* and *A God Who Makes Fire*

One of the awesome things about this Work is that Morgan Daimler sheds new light on Irish Lore. It also brings the stories up to date in modern language as well as it helps fill in some gaps with much needed new translations. This is a must have for anyone interested in the Irish Lore.
Sam 'Bo' Thompson, author of *Metal Never Lies: An Introduction to Metal Magic*

My new favorite reference book! With clearly cited source material, M. Daimler weaves their translation of the Old Irish and Middle Irish texts in an easy-to-follow, comfortable-for-the-eye-and-the-brain format. Personal notes with additional commentary from the author make this feel like they are speaking directly with and not at the reader, much like attending one of their workshops.
Deborah A. Meyerriecks, author of *Macha and the Medic,* co-author of *Living In Magick,* and a contributing author to the Girl God Books anthology series.

Tales of the Tuatha Dé Danann

New Translations of Irish Myths

Volume 1

Morgan Daimler

MOON BOOKS
London, UK
Washington, DC, USA

CollectiveInk

First published by Moon Books, 2025
Moon Books is an imprint of Collective Ink Ltd.,
Unit 11, Shepperton House, 89 Shepperton Road, London, N1 3DF
office@collectiveinkbooks.com
www.collectiveinkbooks.com
www.moon-books.net

For distributor details and how to order please visit the 'Ordering' section on our website.

Text copyright: Morgan Daimler 2024

ISBN: 978 1 80341 916 9
978 1 80341 918 3 (ebook)
Library of Congress Control Number: 2024942261

All rights reserved. Except for brief quotations in critical articles or reviews, no part of this book may be reproduced in any manner without prior written permission from the publishers.

The rights of Morgan Daimler as author have been asserted in accordance with the Copyright, Designs and Patents Act 1988.

A CIP catalogue record for this book is available from the British Library.

Design: Lapiz Digital Services

UK: Printed and bound by CPI Group (UK) Ltd, Croydon, CR0 4YY
Printed in North America by CPI GPS partners

We operate a distinctive and ethical publishing philosophy in all areas of our business, from our global network of authors to production and worldwide distribution.

Contents

All Irish texts within are held in the public domain.
English material translated by Morgan Daimler.

Readers will note that the text includes some spelling variations of names. Old and Middle Irish are nonstandard orthographic languages which means that there was no standardized spelling and it was common to find a range of variations. While I have tried to keep any name within an obvious close relation to itself, I am also trying to stay true to the original texts and their variety. Readers may note that the same name has a sineadh fada (accent mark) over a vowel in one story but not another, such as Etaine and Étaine; this is an example of a normal variation.

For Lora, without whom this book would not exist.

I would like to thank all of my patrons on Patreon for supporting my ongoing translation work and for all of my friends in person and across social media for their support and encouragement.

Ardotraib bennacht co brath

Introduction

In 2015 I began teaching myself Sean- agus Meán-Ghaeilge, Old and Middle Irish, because I had realized that the version of the Cath Maige Tuired I was reading was not an ideal translation. It was the Whitley Stokes version and both included material Stokes had inserted as well as excluded large portions that he had cut out. I found this frustrating and so set out to learn to read it myself so I could know what the material really said.

The more I learned the more I realized the problems with many of the available English translations, most of which were over 100 years old. Translators of that period, like Stokes, would freely add or remove material based on their own opinions and mores as well as omitting material that was considered too difficult to render into English. Additionally, the study of the language has progressed very far from where it was in the late 19th and early 20th century and some terms that weren't known then have been deciphered now. All of this can radically affect the story as it is relayed through the translation.

Older Irish doesn't lend itself to literal translation to English because to an English speaker what is rendered tends to look clunky and redundant, however in altering the material to better suit an English language audience the feel and spirit of the original is, in my opinion, often lost. What we are left with may seem beautiful in English but it may not reflect the original story, only the translator's opinion of the spirit of the original story and that quickly becomes perspective and opinion. My own approach is to stay as close to a literal version as possible, even though that doesn't flow as well in English. I think having the tone of the original is important.

What I'm including here in this text is an assortment of material from Old and Middle Irish that I have translated into English over the last nine years. The English and Irish are integrated, with public domain versions of the older Irish interspersed between my English translation. The material here tends to focus on stories of the Tuatha Dé Danann and the Aos Sidhe as they are a main interest of mine, but otherwise is not intended to be cohesive or offer complete versions of entire mythic cycles. My own approach to translation is more literal and direct than poetic in English. I am also offering a short introduction to many of the stories to help summarize and partially contextualize the various pieces.

This book also includes at least two pieces – Apraid a éolchu Elga and Fothart for trebaib Con Corbb – which have not previously been translated and published in English. I hope that offering them here will be a useful resource for readers. Readers may also note that some of the text is in Latin rather than Irish; this was common for the manuscript material and is usually only a single word or sentence within a wider piece.

It is important to remember, of course, that I am an amateur translator who is doing this out of love for the language; I do not have any formal degree in Old or Middle Irish. Nonetheless I hope that it can be useful to readers and possibly open up new understandings of these texts and stories.

Finally, I want to remind readers that the Irish texts presented here are *not* in modern Irish – Gaeilge Nua – but in older forms of the language. Old and Middle Irish are to modern Irish what Old and Middle English are to modern English, that is similar in some ways but very different in others. Readers and speakers of modern Irish will not necessarily be able to read Old Irish because they are too different; for one example the verb 'see' in Old Irish is ad-cí while modern Irish is feic. I am including the original language texts here for those who are interested in correlating the translation with the original or who are interested in learning for themselves. I have also offered extensive footnoting explaining some of my choices in translation for the same reason.

Chapter 1

The Mythological cycle

Irish mythology is broken down into various sets of stories, referred to as cycles. Chapter 1 contains several translations of stories found within the mythic cycle which focuses on the Tuatha De Danann and to a lesser extent the Aos Sidhe. These stories are interesting from several perspectives and can offer insight into how these beings were understood a millennia ago as well as give us more information about their personalities and activities. The following stories are not arranged in any kind of chronological order, either by when they were written or how they might be ordered consecutively, but are simply organized in what seemed like a logical fashion to me.

De Gabail In tSide
The Taking of the Sídhe[1]

> This story which dates to sometime in the 800's tells us how it is the Tuatha De Danann came to be in the sidhe, some important details about where various members of the Tuatha De reside, and one version of how Oengus came to win Sid in Broga [Newgrange] in this case from the Dagda. It is overall an important story from a cosmological and mythic perspective. The Irish text is from the *Lebar na Núachongbála.*

Boí rí amra for Tuathaib Dea i nHere. Dagan a ainm. Ba mór dí a chumachta, ced la Maccu Miled iar ngabail in tíre. Ar collset Tuatha Dea ith ocus blicht im Maccu Miled. Co ndingsat chairddes in Dagdai. Doessartsaide iarum ith ocus blicht dóib.

There was a marvellous king of the Tuatha Dea in Ireland. Dagda was his name. Great was his power, even in the present time when the Sons of Mil have taken the land, on account of the Tuatha Dea destroying the grain and milk of the Sons of Mil, until they made an alliance with the Dagda. Afterwards he preserves the grain and milk for them.

Ba mór dí a chumachtasom in tan ba rí i tossuch, ocus ba hé fodail inna side do feraib Dea .i. Lug mac Ethnend i sSíd Rodrubán, Ogma i sSíd Aircheltrai, Don Dagdu fessin im Síth Leithet Lachtmaige oí asíd Cnocc Báine. Brú Ruair. Síd in Broga dano ba laiss i tossuch, amal asberat. Do lluid dí in Mac Oac cosin Dagda, do chungid feraind o forodail do chách, ba daltasaide dí do Midir Breg Léith, ocus do Nindid faith.

Great was his power while he was king in the beginning and he distributed the sídhe to the men of the Gods that is Lugh mac Ethne in the sídhe at Rodrubán, Ogma in the sídhe at Aircheltra, the Dagda himself the sídhe Leithet Lachtmaige, sheep-ful the White Mound, Brú Ruair. The sídhe of Broga then was among his at the beginning, as they say. Then the Mac Oc went to Dagda seeking territory but it was all dispersed; he was a foster son to Midir Bri Leith and Nindid the Seer.

"Nimthá duit" ol in Dagda. "Ni tharnaic fodail lemm."

"There is nothing to go to you", said the Dagda. "Everything has been distributed by me."

"Etá dam dí" ol in Mac Ooc. "Cid bia co n-aidchi it trib féin."
Dobreth dosom ón iarum.

"Obtain for me this," said the Mac Oc, "even hospitality with the following night in your own place."

This was given to him afterwards.

"Collá dot daim tra" ol in Dagda.

"Your time as a guest is over,"[2] said the Dagda.

"Uaire doromailt do ré Is menand" olse. "is laa ocus adaig in bith uile. Ocus iss ed on doratad damsa."

"Hours consume a man's time, it is evident," he said. "It is a day and night in life always. And it is the aforementioned I was given."

Luid dó Dagán ass iarum ocus anaid in Macc Oóc ina síd. Amra dano a tír hisin. Ataat tri chrand co torud and do grés, ocus mucc bithbeo fo chossaib ocus mucc fonaithe. Ocus lestar co llind sainemail. Ocus ni erchranand sin uile do grés.

The Dagda went out afterwards and the Mac Oc remained in the sídhe. Wonderful moreover his land there. There were three trees with produce there on them always, and a pig always in life on its feet, and a pig roasted. And a vessel with distinctive drink. And all these things never fail, always.

In Gabal in Dagdai a Luirg
How the Dagda Got His Magic Staff

One of the more important stories in the collection, in my opinion, this tells the tale of the Dagda trying to find a way to save his son Cermad, who had been killed in a fit of jealousy by Lugh. This quest leads the Dagda to find what will become his most signature possession, a staff that can both give and take life. The story, like many in this cycle, dates to the late 8th or early 9th century in the Leabhar Buidhe Leacáin. The Irish text is from Osbom, B., (1927). *How the Dagda Got His Magic Staff.*

"Aed Abaid Essa Ruaid misi .i. dagdia druidechta Tuath De Danann ocus in Ruad Rofhessa Eochaid Ollathair mo tri hanmanna."

"I am Aed Abaid Essa Ruaid that is the good god of sorcery of the Tuatha De Danann and Ruad Rofhessa, Eochaid Ollathair[3] are my three names."

Ocus is amlaid ro bai-sium ocus mac dó aigi fora muin .i. Cermad Minbeoil, ocus adrochairsium a comrag ocus a comlonn la Lug mac Cein la hairdri Erenn, do-chuaidh in Dagda a muinighin a fhessa ocus a fhireolais dus in ticfad anam ina mac, conad airi sin tucad mir ocus tuis ocus lossa ma corp Cermada, ocus tuargaibsium Cermatfora muin, ocus siris an doman fa Cermut, ocus ro-siacht in doman mor soir.

And thus he was and with one of his son's on his back that is Cermad Minbeoil,[4] who had fallen in his combat and his battle with Lugh son of Cein the high king of Ireland, the Dagda put his trust in his knowledge and his experience to see if he could bring the soul [back] in his son, so that around the body of

Cermad where placed myrrh and frankincense and many herbs, and he took Cermad on his back, and he wandered the world with Cermad, and went towards the great world in the east.

Dorecmaingedar triar dósom ag imdecht na conairi ocus na sligead ocus seoid a n-athar accu. Fiarfaigid in Dagdai scela dib, ocus adubradar: "Tri meic aenathar ocus aenmathar sind, ocus seoid ar n-athar acainn aga roind."

He happened upon a trio together on account of journeying the path and the course with the treasures of their father with them. The Dagda asked their story, and they answered: "We are three sons of one father and one mother, and the treasures of our father are shared among us."

"Cred agaib?" bar in Dagdai.

"What do you have?" said the Dagda.

"Lene lorc ocus lumann," bar iadsan.

"A shirt, staff and shield,"[5] they said.

"Cred na buada fuilet forro sin?" bar in Dagdai.

"What is the value that is on them?" said the Dagda.

"An lorg mór sa adchi," ar se, "cenn ailgen aqi ocus cenn ainbthean. Indara cend ag marbad na mbeo, ocus in cenn ele ag tathbeougud na marb."

"The great staff that you see," said one, "a gentle end here and a violent end. One end kills the living, and the other end restores to life the dead."

"Cred in lene ocus in lumann,' ar in Dagdai, 'ocus cred a mbuada?"

"What of the shirt and shield," said the Dagda, "and what are their values?"

"Ante gabus uime in lumann, a roga crotha ocus delba denma, ocus a roga datha, gen bhes ulme. In lene tra, gach cness imma ragha, gan cess gan galor do denum di."

"He that takes on himself the shield, his choice of shape and pure form, and his choice of coloring, while it is on him. The shirt then, every surface that's chosen, without debility without sickness happening to him who wears it."

"Taile in lorg am laimsea," bar in Dagdai. Ocus tucsad ar iasacht in lorg do, ocus ro fhuirmesdarsum in lorg fo tri orro, ocus adrocradar a triur laiss, ocus ro thunius dar in cenn ailgen fora mac, ocus adracht na nertlainti ocus forurim Cermad a laim for a aigid ocus adracht ocus ro sill for in triur marb ro boi ina fhadnaisi.

"Give the staff to my hand," said the Dagda. and they gave the staff to him, and he arranged the staff on the three, and the trio fell by it, and then he put the gentle end on his son, and he bound the full strength and stability on Cermad; his hands to his face he rises, and he gazes on the dead trio there before him.

"Cuich in triur marb sa filet at fiadnasi?" ar Cermad.

"Who are the three dead here before me?" said Cermad.

"Triar dorala damsa," bar in Dagdai. "ocus seoida n-athar acu ga comroind. Tucsadar iasacht dun lurig damsa, ocus ro marbusa iad dun dara cind, ocus do thathbheoaiges tussu dun cind ele."

"Three who I met," said the Dagda. "and the treasures of their father where with them for dividing. They gave the loan of the staff to me, and I killed them with the second end, and restored you to life with the other end."

"Dursan in gnim sin," an Cermad, "in ni dia tainic mo bheougudsa gan a tathbeougudsum de."

"Misfortune in doing that," said Cermad, "when that which restored me to life did not restore them to life as well."

Fuirmis in Dagda forrosan in luirg, ocus adractadar na nertslainti an triar brathar.

"Nach fedabair bar marbad," ar se, "do bar luirg fesin?"

The Dagda settled the staff on them, and the three brothers arose in strong health.

"Do you know you were dead," said he, "by your staff itself?"

"Rofedamar," ar siad, "ocus ro imris baegal oruind."

"We know," said they, "and we dispute being slain off guard."

"Agamsa ata eolus bar luirgi," an in Dagdai, "ocus tugus bar tri hanmana daib, ocus tabraidsi iasacht na luirgi damsa co hErind."

"I have knowledge of the staff," said the Dagda, "and have given you three your lives; give the loan of the staff to me to go to Ireland."

"Cred is chuir no is tennta duinn fris immar lurig do thorachtain duinn?"

"What guarantees or trust for us that the staff will come to us?"

"Grian ocus esga, muir ocus tir, acht co marbursa mo naimdi di ocus gu tathbeoaider mu chairdh". Ocus tuccad dosum iasacht na luirgi fan coma sin.

"Sun and moon, sea and land, only that it kills my enemies and brings to life my friends." And they gave to him the loan of the staff to remain with him with that concession.

"Cindus roindfimid nada set fil againd?" ar siat.

"How shall we divide the treasures we have left?" they said.

"Dias agaib fana sedaib aenfer gan ni, nogo ria tim chell chugi."

"The treasures to remain with the two, one man without any, until his time is yielded to him."

Is ann sin tucsom in luirg sin i nErind ocus a mac, ocus ro niarb a naimdi di, ocus do thathbeoaig a chairdi, ocus do gabastair rigi nErenn a los na luirgi sin.

Then he took the staff to Ireland and his son, and killed his enemies, and brought to life his friends, and he took the kingship of Ireland with the ends of that staff.

"Arai sin," ar se. "is mac dun Dagdai sin misi ocus gach a raibi do draidecht d' fhisidecht aigi, ata agamsa, ocus gach an fhogluim d'eolus ag an tsluag ut, ata agamsa sin, ocus racaid misi leatsu, a macaim, do thoigi in tsegaind ut guro impaidher a ranna ocus a faebra," et reliqua.

"On account of this," said he, "a son of the Dagda am I and each magic and wizardry that he had, I have, and every wisdom and knowledge from the host, I have, and I declare I will go with you, my boy, to houses of champions yonder sharp commanding portions and his sharp-blades," etc.

Buach ingen Dairi Duind, ben Loga meic Eithlenn, is ma gnais dochuaidh Cermad mac in·Dagdai, conad inn ro marbad Cermad la Lug.

Buach daughter of Dairi Donn, wife of Lugh, son of Eithlenn, had intercourse with Cermad son of the Dagda, and so Cermad was slain by Lugh.

Tuath De Danand na Set soim
The Treasures of the Tuatha De Danann

A piece that is partially prose and partially poem, 'Tuath De Danand na Set soim' describes the Tuatha de Danann before they came to Ireland, their greatest magical treasures, and where they obtained them. The Irish text is from Hull, V., (1930) *The Four jewels of the Tuatha Dé Danann*. Zeitschrift für Celtische Philologie. vol 18.

Ceithri cathracha i r-robadar Tuatha De Danand ic foglaim fheasa ocus druidechta, uair is fis ocus druidecht ocus diabaldanacht ro fhogain doib. it e-seo anmanna na cathrach .i. Failias, ocus Findias, ocus Goirias, ocus Murias. Ocus is a Failias tucad in Lia Fail, fil i Temraig, no gesed fo cech rig no gebead h-Erind . A Gorias tucad in claidheb bai ic Nuadaid. A Findias tucad sleg Loga. A Murias tucadcoire in Dagda.

The Tuatha De Danann were in four cities learning wisdom and Druidism, a time of learning and magic and diabolic arts on them. These were the names of the cities that is Failias, and Findias, and Goirias, and Murias. And out of Failias was brought the Lia Fail, taken to Tara, it cried out under every king who would take Ireland. Out of Gorias was brought the sword that was Nuada's. Out of Findias was brought the spear of Lugh. Out of Murias was brought the cauldron of the Dagda.

Ceithri fiseda badar isna cathrachaib sin .i. Fessus bai h-i Failias, Esrus bai ic Gorias, Uscias bai a Findias, Semias bai a Murias. Is aco sin rofoglaimsed Tuatha De Danand fis ocus eolus. Sleg Loga, ni gebthea cath fria na fris inti a m-bid laim. Claidheb Nuadad, ni thernad neach ara n-dergad. O da berthea asa thindtig bodba, ni gebti fris inti a m-bid laim. Coiri in Dagda, ni teigead dam dimdach uad . An Lia Fail, fil i Temraig, ni labrad acht fa rig Erenn.

Four magicians there were in these cities that is Fessus was in Failias, Esrus was at Gorias, Uscias was in Findias, Semias was in Murias. The Tuatha De Danann learned from them wisdom and knowledge. The spear of Lugh, no battle could be sustained against whoever had it in his hand. The sword of Nuada, none escapes who is reddened by it. When taken from its attacking sheath, no conquest against whoever had it in his hand. The cauldron of the Dagda, no company went displeased from it. And the Lia Fail, in Tara, didn't speak but under a king of Ireland.

Ad-beraid, imorro, aroile do seanchaidib conid a n-dluim ciach tistais Tuatha De Danann i n-Erind. Ocus ni h-ead on, acht a longaib namorloinges tangadar, ocus ro loiscsed a longa uili iar tuidecht i n-Erind. Ocus is don dluim ciach bai dib side, at-dubradar aroile conid a n-dluim chiach tangadar. Ocus ni h-ead iar fir . Ar is iad so da fhochaind ara r' loiscsead a longa na r' fhagbaidis fine Fomra iad do fodail forro, ocus na ro thisad Lug do cosnum rigi fri Nuagaid. Conid doib do chan in seanchaid:

It's told, however, otherwise by historians that with gushes of mists went the Tuatha De Danann in Ireland. This was not so, but they came in many ships, and they burned all their ships after they came in Ireland. And from this gushing mist that rose from them, some said it was in mist they came. This was not true. These are the two reasons they burned their ships: the group of Fomorians would not find them and raid upon them, and Lug could not come opposing the kingship against Nuada. About them the historian said this:

Tuath De Danand na set soim.
Cait a fuaradar fogloim?

Do rangadar suigecht slan
A n-druigecht , a n-diabaldan.
Iardanel find, faith co feib,
Mac Nemid, mac Agnomain ,
D'ar mac baeth Beothach bertach,
Ba loech leothach, lanfhertach.
Clanna Beothaich, — beoda a m-blad —
Rangadar sluag niath nertmar,
Iar snim is iar toirrsi truim,
Lin a loingsi co Lochluinn.
Ceithri cathracha, — clu cert —
Gabsad a rem co ronert.
Do curdis comlann co cas
Is d'foglaim a fireolas.
Failias ocus Goiriasglan,
Findias, Murias na morgal,
O maitea madmann amach,
Anmanna na n-ardchathrach.

Tuatha De Danann of the valuable treasures.
Where did they attain wisdom?
They drew in complete
Their Druidism, their diabolism.
Fair Iardanel, prophet of distinction,
Son of Nemed, son of Agnomain,
His reckless son was active Beothach,[6] who was a warrior of wounding, full of miracles.
Beothach's children, — fortunate their triumphs —
A host of capable warriors came,
After battle and after sad weariness,
With all their ships to Lochluinn.
Four cities, — deserved their fame —
Held primacy with great strength.

Always warriors in contention with sorrow
They were studying truth and knowledge.
Failias and pure Goirias,
Findias, Murias of great valour,
From which battles retreat outwards,
The names of the high cities.

Morfis ocus Erus ard,
Uscias is Semiath sirgarg,
Re n-garmand, — luag a leasa —
Anmann suad a s-sarfeasa .
Morfis fili a Failias fen,
Esrus a Gorias, germen,
Semiath a Murias, dind dias,
Uscias fili find Findias.
Ceithri h-aisceda leo anall,
D'uaislib Tuaithi De Danand:
Claideb, cloch, coiri cumal,
Sleag ri h-aidid ardcurad.
Lia Fail a Failias anall,
Gesed fo rigaib Erend.
Claideb lama Loga luidh
A Goirias, — roga rocruid.
A Findias tar fairrgi i fad
Tucad sleg nemneach Nuadat.
A Murias, main adbol oll,
Coiri in Dagda na n-ardglond.
Ri Nime, Ri na fer fand,
Ro-m-aince, Rig na rigrand,
Fear ca fuil fulang na fuath,
Ocus cumang na caemtuath.
Tuata.
Finit

Morfis and lofty Erus,
Uscias and Semiath always fierce,
To call them, — a source of value —
Their names, exceedingly wise,
Morfis was the poet of Failias itself,
Esrus out of Gorias, sharp-mouthed,
Semiath out of Murias, pleasant points,
Uscias the poet of fair Findias.
Four gifts with them from beyond,
The noble Tuatha De Danann:
Sword, stone, champion's cauldron,
King's spear violent death of great heroes.
Stone of Fal from Falias thither.
It cries out under kings of Ireland.
The sword moves to Lugh's hand
Out of Goirias, — a choice of wealth.
Out of Findias across the wide ocean
Was brought the deadly spear of Nuada.
Out of Murias, a vast, great treasure,
The Cauldron of the Dagda of heroic deeds.
King of heaven, King of helpless men,
May he protect me, King of kingly portions,
Man whose blood holds out against spectres,
and strength of the noble people.
Tuatha.
The end.

Aislinge Oenguso
Oengus's Dream

A wide-ranging tale of Oengus, his parents the Dagda and Bóinn, and the Aos sidhe, which tells us how Oengus met and eventually gained his love Caer Ibormeith. This piece contains a great deal of information about several important mythic figures as well as about the magic of the Otherworld more generally.

The Irish of this version dates to the 1517 Egerton manuscript 1782, folio 70b, but the tale itself is referenced 400 years prior as a pre-tale to the Táin Bó Cúailgne, indicating that the age of the story is considerably older than the surviving text. Unfortunately, we don't have any earlier versions of the tale that have survived, to my knowledge. The Irish text is from Shaw, F., (1934) *Aislinge Óenguso.*

Boí Óengus in n-aidchi n-aili inna chotlud. Co n-accae ní, in n-ingin cucci for crunn síuil dó. Is sí as áilldem ro boí i n-Ére. Luid Óengus do gabáil a l-lámae dia tabairt cucci inna imdai. Co n-accae ní; fo-sceinn úad opunn. Nícon fitir cia árluid h-úad. Boí and co arabárach. Nípo slán laiss a menmae. Do-génai galar n-dó in delb ad-condairc cen a h-accaldaim. Nícon luid biad inna béolu. Boí and do aidchi dano aithirriuch. Co n-accae timpán inna láim as bindem boíe. Sennid céol n- dó. Con-tuil friss. Bíid and co arabárach. Nícon ro-proindig dano arabárach.

Óengus was sleeping when he saw a desirable thing. He saw something, the girl appearing to him while he was in bed, and she the most desirable in Ireland. Óengus went to seize her hand to take her to him in his bed. Then he saw nothing; he jumped up from surprise. He did not know what she has flown from. He was there until the next day. Not healthy was he because of his thoughts. He became sick from seeking the figure he wanted to speak to. He did not take food in his mouth. Moreover, he saw her at night again. He saw her with a timpán in her hand that was melodious. She played music on it, to him, there with him until the next day. However, she was not with him before his first meal the next day.

Blíadain lán dó os sí occa aithigid fon séol sin condid corastar i sergg. Nícon epert fri nech. F-a-ceird i sergg íarum ocus ní fitir nech cid ro m-boí. Do-ecmalldar legi Érenn. Nícon fetatar-som cid ro m-boí asendud. Ethae co Fíngen, liaig Conchobuir. Do-tét-side cucci. Ad-gninad-som i n-aigid in duini a n-galar no bíth for ocus ad-gninad din dieid no théiged din tig a l-lín no bíth co n-galar and.

A full year thus while she visited about his bed there so that he fell into a wasting sickness. He did not tell anyone. He exhibited a wasting sickness later and there was no one who knew what was with him. The healers of Ireland gathered together. They did not know what ailed him in the end. One was sent to Fíngen, healer of Conchobuir. He went towards him. He discovered in studying the man the sickness or wound on him and he discovered from the smoke or people going from the house there was a sickness there.

Atn-gládastar for leith.

"Ate! nítat béodai do imthechta", ol Fíngen, "Sercc écmaise ro carais."

He addressed him apart.

"Indeed! Not active are your wanderings", said Fíngen, "You greatly love an absent beloved."

"Ad-rumadar mo galar form", ol Óengus.

"Do-rochar i n-dochraidi ocus ní rolámar a epirt fri nech", ol Fíngen.

"You have judged my sickness on me", said Óengus.

"Falling in this unseemliness and greatly burdened you told no one", said Fíngen.

"Is fír deit", ol Óengus. "Do-m-ánaic ingen álaind in chrotha as áilldem i n-Ére co n-écusc derscaigthiu. Timpán inna l-láim, conid senned dam cach n-aidchi."

"It's truth to you,"[7] said Óengus. "A beautiful maiden comes in the most desirable form in Ireland with an excellent appearance. A timpán in her hand, playing for me each night."

"Ní báe", ol Fíngen, "do-rogad duit cairdes frie; ocus foítter úait cossin m-Boinn, cot máthair, co tuidich dot accaldaim."

"No matter", said Fíngen, "Friendship for her was chosen to you; and let you send for the Boínn, your mother, to come to speak to you."

Tíagair cuicce. Tic iarum in Boann. "Bíu oc frepaid ind fir-se", ol Fíngen, "d-an-ánaic galar n-ainchis".

Ad-fíadot a scéla don Boinn.

Someone was sent to her. Then came the Boínn.

"I am healing this man", said Fíngen, "to whom came a serious sickness".

Then they told the story to the Boínn.

"Bíd a freccor céill dia máthair", ol Fíngen. "D-an-ánaic galar n-ainchis; ocus timchelltar h-úait Ériu uile, dús in n-étar h-úait ingen in chrotha so ad-condairc do macc".

"Now will his attending be by his mother", said Fíngen. "To him came a serious sickness; and you must travel around all Ireland, to see if you can obtain a maiden in the form seen by your son".

Bíid oc suidiu co cenn m-blíadnae. Nícon frith ní ba chosmail di. Is iar sin con-gairther Fíngen doib aithirriuch.

"Nícon frith cobair isindísiu", ol Boann.

She did this until the end of a year. Nothing was found similar to her. After that Fíngen gathered them together.

"Nothing of help in this matter was found", said Boínn.

As-bert Fíngen: "Foítter cossin n-Dagdae tuidecht do accaldaim a maicc".

Tíagair cossin n-Dagdae. Ticc-side aithirriuch. "Cid diandom-chomgrad?"

Fíngen spoke: "Send someone to the Dagda that he may help his son".

Someone was sent to the Dagda. Then came the aforementioned. "Why have I been called?"

"Do airli do maicc", ol in Boann. "Is ferr duit a chobair. Is liach a dul immudu. At-tá i siurgg. Ro car seircc écmaise ocus ní roachar a chobair".

"To advise your son", said the Boínn. "It is better to you to help him. His manner is sorrowful. He is in a wasting sickness. He loves an absent love and no help has been reached".

"Cia torbae mo accaldam?" ol inDagdae. "Ní móo mo éolas in- dáthe-si".

"Móo écin", ol Fíngen. "Is tú rí síde n-Érenn; ocus tíagar úaib co Bodb, ríg síde Muman, ocus is deilm a éolas la h-Érinn n-uili".

"What use calling me?" said the Dagda. "Not greater my knowledge than yours".

"Greater certainly", said Fíngen. "You are the king of the sidhe[8] of Ireland; and let someone go from you to Bodb, king of the sídhe of Muman, and the fame of his knowledge is in all Ireland".

Ethae co suide. Feraid-side fáilti friu. "Fo chen dúib", ol Bodb, "a muinter in Dagdai".

"Is ed do-roachtmar".

"Scéla lib?" ol Bodb.

"Atáat linni: Óengus macc in Dagdai i siurgg dá blíadnae."

Someone is sent. He welcomes them. "A nod to you,"[9] said Bodb, "people of the Dagda"."It is reached".

"What story with you?" said Bodb.

"This way with us: Óengus son of the Dagda in a wasting sickness for two years."

"Cid táas?" ol Bodb.

"Ad-condairc ingin inna chotlud. Nícon fetammar i n-Ére cia h-airm i tá ind ingen ro char ocus ad-condairc. Timmarnad duit ón Dagdae co comtastar h-úait fond Érinn ingen in chrotha-sa ocus ind écuisc."

"How is this?" said Bodb.

"He saw a maiden in his sleep. We do not know in Ireland where is the maiden who he loved and saw. You are ordered by the Dagda to seek through Ireland a maiden in this form and this likeness."

"Con- díastar", ol Bodb, "ocus étar dál blíadnae friumm co fessur fis scél".

Do-lluid cinn blíadnae co tech m-Buidb co Síd Ar Femen.

"To-imchiullus Érinn n-uili co fuar in n-ingen oc Loch Bél Dracon oc Crottaib Cliach", ol Bodb.

"It will be searched", said Bodb, "and obtain for me a meeting at the end of a year to know the story".

He came after a year to the house of Bodb at Sídhe Al Femen.

"I made a circuit of all Ireland until I found the maiden at Loch Bél Dracon at Crottaib Cliach", said Bodb.

Tíagair úaidib dochum in Dagdai. Ferthair fáilte friu. "Scéla lib?" ol in Dagdae.

"Scéla maithi; fo-fríth ind ingen in chrotha-so as-rubartaid. Timmarnad duit ó Bodb. Táet ass Óengus linni a dochum dús in n-aithgne in n-ingin, conda accathar."

Someone was sent by them to the Dagda. They were welcomed by them. "News with you?" said the Dagda.

"Good news; the girl of this appearance that you sought is found. You have been summoned by Bodb. Bring out Óengus with us to see if he recognizes the maiden, when he sees her."

Brethae Óengus i carput co m-boí oc Síd Al Femen. Fled mór lassin ríg ara ciunn. Ferthae fáilte friss. Bátar trí láa ocus teora aidchi ocond fleid.

"Tair ass trá", ol Bodb, "dús in n-aithgne in n-ingin conda aiccther. Ci ad-da-gnoe, ní-s cumcaim-si a tabairt acht ad-n-da-cether namá."

Óengus was carried in a chariot until he was at Síd Al Femen. A great feast was for them with the king at the head. He was welcomed. They were three days and three nights at the feast.

"Come out of it then", said Bodb, "to see if you recognize the maiden when you see her. Who you may recognize, no power have I to give her to you except you may see her only."

To-lotar íarum co m-bátar oc Loch. Co n-accatar inna tri cóecta ingen macdacht. Co n-accatar in n-ingin n-etarru. Ní tacmuictis inna h-ingena dí acht coticci a gualainn. Slabrad airgdide eter cach dí ingin. Muince airgdide imma brágait fadisin ocus slabrad di ór forloiscthiu. Is and as-bert Bodb: "In n-aithgén in n-ingen n-ucut?"

"Aithgén écin", ol Óengus.

They came later until they were at the Loch. They saw there girls of marriageable age in three groups of fifty. They saw the maiden among them. The girls didn't reach only as far as her shoulders. A silver chain was between each two girls. A silver collar around her throat itself and a chain of gold shining on her. And there spoke Bodb: "Do you recognize the maiden yonder?"

"I recognize her certainly", said Óengus.

"Ní-m thá-sa cumacc deit", ol Bodb, "bas móo."

"Ní báe són", ol Óengus, "ém; óre as sí ad-condarc; ní cumcub a breith in fecht-so.Cuich ind ingen-sa, a Buidb?" ol Óengus.

"Ro-fetar écin", ol in Bodb, "Caer Ibormeith, ingen Ethail Anbuail a s-Síd Úamain i crích Connacht".

"I have no more power for you", said Bodb, "a great measure."

"That is no matter", said Óengus, "indeed; because it is she I saw; I have no power to bring her forth on the journey. Who is the maiden, oh Bodb?" said Óengus.

"I know certainly", said Bodb, "Caer Ibormeith, daughter of Ethail Anbuail from Sídhe Úamain in the district of Connacht".

Do-comlat ass íarum Óengus ocus a muinter dochum a críche. Téit Bodb laiss co n-árlastar in n-Dagdae ocus in m-Boinn oc Bruig Maicc ind Óicc. Ad-fíadat a scéla doib ad-fídatar doib amail m-boíe eter cruth ocus écoscc amail ad-condarcatar. Ocus ad-fídatar a h-ainm ocus ainm a h-athar ocus a senathar.

Óengus and his people departed then to the region. He brought Bodb with him to speak to the Daghda and the Boínn at Bruig

Maicc ind Óicc.[10] He told his story to them relating to them her form between shape and appearance as they had seen. And told her name and her father's name and her grandfather.

"Ní ségdae dúnn", ol in Dagdae, "ná cumcem do socht."

"Aní bad maith duit, a Dagdai", olBodb. "Eircc dochum n-Ailella ocus Medbae ar is leo bíid inna cóiciud ind ingen."

"Not fortunate to us", said the Daghda, "no control have we over your gloom."

"There is some good to you, oh Daghda", said Bodb. "Go to Ailill and Medb because the maiden is near them in their region."

Téit in Dagdae co m-boí i tírib Connacht, trí fichit carpat a lín. Ferthae fáilte friu lassin víg ocus in rígnai. Bátar sechtmain láin oc fledugud íar sin im chormann doib. "Cid immu-b-rácht?" ol in rí.

The Dagda goes so he is in the land of Connacht, three twenties [60] of chariots in his company. Welcome was given to them by the king and queen. They were a complete week drinking and feasting after that there with them.

"Why have you come?" said the king.

"At-tá ingen lat-su it ferunn'", ol in Dagdae, "ocus ro-s car mo macc-sa, ocus do-rónad galar dó. Do-dechad-sa cuccuib dús in-da-tartaid don macc."

"Cuich?" ol Ailill.

"Ingen Ethail Anbuail."

"Ní linni a cumacc", ol Ailill ocus Medb. "Dia cuimsimmis do-bérthae dó."

"There is a maiden in your country'", said the Dagda, "and my son has loved her, and been in a sickness. We have come hence to find out if you can give her to our son."

"Who?" said Ailill.

"The daughter of Ethail Anbuail."

"The power is not with us", said Ailill and Medb. "If we were able to, we would obtain her for him."

"Ani for-maith -congairther rí in t-síde cuccuib", ol in Dagdae.

Téit rechtaire Ailella cucci. "Timmarnad duit ó Ailill ocus Meidb dul dia n-accaldaim".

"Ní reg-sa", ol sé. "Ní tibér mo ingin do macc in Dagdai". Fásagar co h-Ailill anísin. "Ní étar fair a thuidecht; ro-fitir aní dia con-garar."

"Ní báe', ol Ailill, "do-rega-som ocus do-bértar cenna a laech laiss."

"It is best to call the king of the sídhe to you", said the Dagda.

Ailill's steward goes to him. "A command to you from Ailill and Medb to go speak with them".

"I will not go", he says. "I will not give my daughter to the Dagda's son".

Notice was given to Ailill of this. "Not great his arrival; he knows why he was commanded"

"No matter", said Ailill, "He will go and the heads of his warriors will be brought with him."

Íar sin cot-éirig teglach n-Ailella ocus muinter in Dagdai dochum in t-síde. Inrethat a síd n-uile. Do-sm-berattrí fichtea cenn ass ocus in ríg co m-boí i Crúachnaib i n-ergabáil.

Is íarum as-bert Ailill fri h-Ethal n-Anbuail: "tabair do ingin do macc in Dagdai."

"Ni cumcaim", ol sé. "Is móo a cumachtae in- dó."

Then arose Ailill's household and the people of the Dagda to go to the sídhe. They laid waste to the entire sídhe. They carried off three-twenties [60] of heads out of it and the king with them to Crúachan in captivity.

Afterward Ailill said to Ethal n-Anbuail: "Give your daughter to the Dagda's son."

"I have not the power", said he. "Her power is greater than mine."

"Ced cumachtae mór fil lee?" ol Ailill.

"Ní anse; bíid i n-deilb éuin cach la blíadnai, in m-blíadnai n-aili i n-deilb duini."

"Ci-ssí blíadain m-bís i n-deilb éuin?" ol Ailill.

"Ní lemm-sa a mrath", ol a h-athair.

"Do chenn dít", ol Ailill, "mani-n-écis-ni."

"Níba sia cucci dam-sa", ol sé.

"What greater power is with her?" said Ailill.

"Not hard; she is in the form of a bird each other year, in the second year in the form of a person."

"What year is she in the form of a bird?" said Ailill.

"She will not be betrayed by me", said her father.

"Your head from you", said Ailill, "Unless you tell us."

"At-bérsa", ol sé; "is lérithir sin ro-n gabsaid occai. In t-samuin-se as nessam bieid i n-deilb éuin oc Loch Bél Dracon, ocus ad-cichsiter sain-éuin lee and, ocus bieit trí cóecait géise n-impe; ocus at-tá aurgnam lemm-sa doib."

"Ni báe lemm-sa iarum," ol in Dagdae, "óre ro-fetar a h-aicned do-s-uc-so".

"I will no longer hold it with me", he said. "I will tell", he said; "you are diligently engaged in seeking her. The Samhain near this she will be in the form of a bird at Loch Bél Dracon,[11] You will see special birds with her there and there will be three fifties (150) of swans about her; and I have feasting preparations with me for them." "No matter to me then" said the Dagda, "because you know her essence you can fulfill this".

Do-gníther íarum cairdes leu .i. Ailill ocus Ethal ocus in Dagdae ocus soírthair Ethal ass. Celebraid in Dagdae doib. Ticc in Dagdae dia thig ocus ad-fét a scéla dia macc. "Eirc immon samuin as nessam co Loch Bél Dracon con-da-garae cuccut dind loch".

Later a friendship was made by them, that is Ailill and Ethal and the Dagda, and a surety was given to Ethal. The Dagda took his leave of them. The Dagda went to his house and related the story to his son. "Go around Samhain near to Loch Bél Dracon and you can call to her from the lake".

Téit in Macc Óc co m-boí oc Loch Bél Dracon. Co n-accae trí cóecta én find forsind loch cona slabradaib airgdidib co caírchesaib órdaib imma cenna. Boí Óengus i n-deilb doínachta for brú ind locha. Con-gair in n-ingin cucci. "Tair dom accaldaim, a Chaer."

"Cia do-m-gair?" ol Caer. "Cotot-gair Óengus."

"Regait diandom fhoíme ar th' inchaib co tís a l-loch mofhrithisi."

"Fo-t-sisiur", ol sé.

The Macc Óc went there by Loch Bél Dracon. He saw three fifties (150) of white birds on the lake with silver chains with golden ringlets on their heads. Óengus was in the form of a person by the edge of the lake. He called the maiden towards him "Come and speak to me, oh Caer."

"Who calls to me?" said Caer.

"Óengus calls to you."

"Give your word on your reputation I may return back to the lake."

"I accept", said he.

Téiti cucci. Fo-ceird-sium dí láim forrae. Con-tuilet i n-deilb dá géise co timchellsat a l-loch fo thrí conná bed ní bad meth n-enech dó-som. To-comlat ass i n-deilb dá én find co m-batar ocin Bruig Maicc in Óicc, ocus chechnatar cocetal cíuil co corastar inna dóini i súan trí láa ocus teora n-aidche. Anais laiss ind ingen íar sin.

She went towards him. He put two arms on her. They slept in the form of two swans and then surrounding the lake for three rounds so there was no failure of his honor to him. They went out in the form of two white birds until they were at Bruig Maicc in Óicc,[12] and singing a song musically threw the people into a magical sleep for three days and three nights. The maiden abided with him there afterwards.

Is de sin ro boí cairdes in Maicc Óic ocus Ailella ocus Medbae. Is de sin do-cuaid Óengus, tricha cét, co Ailill ocus Meidb do tháin inna m-bó a Cúailnge.

Conid 'De Aislingiu Óenguso maicc in Dagdai' ainm in scéuil sin isin Táin Bó Cúailnge.

Then there was friendship between the Maicc Óic and Ailill and Medb. This is the explanation of Óengus's thirty hundred [3,000], with Ailill and Medb at the cattle raid of Cúailnge.

So that 'The Dream of Oengus son of the Dagda' is the name of this story in the Táin Bó Cúailnge

Tomus tighe mec ind Ócc
The Measure of the House of Mac Ind Óg

A short poetic piece describing the home of Oengus, which may be assumed to be Sid in Broga [Newgrange]. The Irish text is from Harleian MS 5280, fo 74a.

Tomus tighe mec ind Ócc,
fót cen bine buidnib sét,
etir dá fraigid rosícht,
mó secht traigid, mó secht cét.
Cethri dorais ind cen brón,
bith oc ól tria bitha sir,
turib ciprib, úair is caem,
cóel fo tuighib d'itib én.
Dabuch deargiubair mór lucht,
slóg óss a ucht cen nach socht,
suide fichet co ba secht,
coire cert ocht fichet torc.

The measure of the house of [Oengus] Mac ind Óc,
a territory without fault, warrior band's treasure,
declared between its two walls,
more than seven feet, more than 700.
Four doors at the edges, without sorrow,
land engaged in revelry through all time,
towers of cypress, because they are fitting,[13]wattling under thatching of bird's wings.
A vat of red yew-wood – great its contents –
A host over it, the interior without any rest,
The aforementioned twenty times seven cows
a proper cauldron [for] eight-score warriors

Tochmarc Étaine
The Wooing of Etain

Another very important story within the corpus, the Tochmarc Etaine offers an alternative version of how Oengus wins the Brugh, this time with him winning it from his mother's husband Elcmar with the help of his father the Dagda. Oengus is fostered with his brother, Midir and through a series of events ends up obligated to obtain a second wife for Midir which he does but with rather disastrous consequences. The Irish version I was able to access is only a partial excerpt of the wider story so I am offering a summary of the sections that I couldn't find in the original language followed by the translation.

The story is preserved in a 12th and 16th century manuscript but has been dated based on the language used to between the 8th and 9th centuries.

The Irish text picks up after a gap. Previous to this gap we learn that the Dagda had fathered a son with the wife of Elcmar and sent the child to foster with Midir, who by some accounts was also a son of the Dagda. The child, Oengus Mac Oc, fosters with Midir, believing Midir to be his father; when he finally asks who his real father is Midir takes him to the Dagda and asks that he be given land and formal acknowledgement. The Dagda acknowledges Oengus as his son, and tells him of a way to trick Elcmar out of possession of the Brugh na Boyne, which Oengus subsequently does.

Later Midir comes to visit Oengus on Samhain and sees two groups of boys fighting as Elcmar looks on in the distance; fearing Elcmar might cause trouble with Oengus if he goes out Midir volunteers to separate the boys. In the process his eye is put out by a stick that is thrown. Oengus calls on Dian Cecht to heal the eye, which he does, but Midir then refuses to stay and visit. He will only remain if Oengus gets him three things: an expensive chariot, a fine cloak, and the hand of Etain the most beautiful maiden in Ireland who is the daughter of a king of Ulster. Oengus can only secure Etain with the Dagda's help by meeting her father's demands to clear 12 plains, creating 12 rivers, and paying her father Etain's weight in gold and silver.

Oengus brings Etain to Midir and they are wed but he warns his foster father that he must be very careful around the jealousy of Fuamnach, who had been raised by a Druid and knew powerful magic. Oengus is concerned because he has promised to keep Etain safe. Midir doesn't listen though and after arriving back at his home Fuamnach transforms Etain into a pool of water, then flees. Eventually from the pool comes a worm who turns into a purple fly. Midir loves the fly as well as he had loved Etain in her human form, and Fuamnach learns of this and returns, using a blast of wind to carry Etain away and throw her about Ireland for seven years. Finally, she lands on Oengus's cloak and he recognizes her, offering her a welcome into his own home.

The Irish text is from the *Lebor na hUidre.*

[starting after gap] *a thaigi ocus a gríanan co senistrib solsib fri techt ass ocus tobreth tlacht corcra impe ocus imchuirthe in gríanán sin lasin Mac Óc cach leth no théged ocus ba and contuiled cach n-aidchi occa chomaitecht do airec menman conda tanic a sult ocus a feth. ocus no línta in gríanán sin do lubib boladmaraib ingantaib combo de forberedsi di bolod ocus blath na lubi sainemail logmar.*

[starting after gap] his household and his crystal bower with a bright window for her going out and returning in. A purple covering was about her and the bower is brought there by Mac Óc each day with affection and he sleeps each night attending her until she found confidence and until she regained her cheerfulness and her tranquillity. And the bower was filled with fragrant wonderful herbs she subsists on both the scent and flowers of the excellent precious herbs.

Atchúas do Fuamnaig a ngrád ocus a mmíad doratad di lasin Mac Óc. Asbert Fuamnach fri Midir "congarar deit do dalta co ndernsai chorai frib dib línaib ocus co ndechos for iarair Etaíne."

Fuamnach heard of his affection and the honor given her by Mac Óc. Fuamnach said to Midir "Call for your foster-son with agreed peace between you both and without a difference in seeking Etaín."

Dotháet techt co Mac nÓc o Midir ocus luidsi día acallaim ocus dolluid Fuamnach timchell calléic co mboí isin Bruig ocus tobertin n-athaig cétnae fo Etaín conda bert asa gríanán forin fúamain forsa rabi ríam co cend .uii. mbliadna fo Herind conda timart athach gaíthe ar thrógi ocus lobrai conda corastár for cléthe tige la Ultu i mbátár oc ól co torchair isin n-airdig n-óir ro boí for láim mná Etair in chathmiled o Inbiur Cichmaine a coiciud Choncobair conda sloicside lasa loim gabais asind lestur co mbentai di suidiu foa broind combo ingen iar tain. Dobreth ainm di .i. Etain ingen Étair. Di bliadain déc ar mili trá o gein tuissech Etaini o Ailill cosa ngein ndedenach o Étur.

Mac nÓc went to the house with Midir and when he was conversing Fuamnach went around meanwhile there to the Brug and puts the same blast of wind over Etaín which carries her away from the bower and from her garment, on a time ever of conflict for seven years around Ireland so that the gust of wind drove her in misery and weakness until she landed on the house posts of Ulster where warriors were with drink and she was thrown into the gold cup that was for the hand of the woman of Etair, wife of the champion of Inbiur Cichmaine in a territory of Choncobair, who she swallows with a sip taken out of the vessel with a strike she arises from it that she [Etain] was under her womb and was her daughter after that time. The name she bore from that is Etain daughter of Étair. One thousand twelve years then from the first birth of Etain from Ailill until the final birth from Étar.

Alta iarom Etain oc Inbiur Chichmuini la hEtar ocus .l. ingen impe di ingenaib tússech ocus ba hesseom noda biathad ocus no n-eted ar chomaitecht Etaini a ingini do gres. Lá n-and doib a n-ingenaib uilib isind inbiur oca fothrocud co n-accatar in marcach isa mmag cucu dond usciu. Ech dond tuagmar foran forlethan casmongach caschairchech foa suidiu. sídhalbrat uaine hi filliud immi. Ocus léne fo derginliud imbi. Ocus eo óir ina brut rosaiged a gúalaind for cach leth. Scíath argdidi co n-imbiul oir imbi fora muin. Scíatrach argit and. Ocus tul n-oir fair. Ocus sleg coicrind co fethan óir impi o irlond co cró ina laim. Folt findbudi fair co hetan. Sníthe óir fria étan conná teilged a folt fo agid. Assisedar sist forsin purt oc deiscin na n-ingen Ocus ro charsat na ingena uili. conid and asbertsom in laid seo sís.

Afterwards Etain was at Inbiur Chichmuini with Etar, that is the girl was with daughters of premiere horsemen about her and he was the one who fed and nicely clothed them to attend his daughter Etain at her work. One day it happened to them that the girls on this occasion were at a river-mouth and were washing when they saw a horseman on the plain from the noble waters. A brown horse splendidly arched, broad above curly-maned curly-tailed beneath the aforementioned. A folding green cloak bending around him. And a red ornamented shirt on him. And gold brooch on the cloak reaches his shoulders on each side. A silver shield with a gold border on it on his neck. A shield-strap of silver and a shield-boss of gold on it. And a spear bordered with gold bands on it from the butt of the spear to the hoop of the lance in his hand. Yellow hair on him to his forehead. A headband of gold against his forehead which keeps his hair from his face. He stops for a time there in that place gazing at the girl and all the girls loved him. So then he spoke the poem here;

Etain indiu sund amne oc Síd Ban Find iar n-Albai eter maccaib beccaib di for brú Inbir Cíchmuini. Is hí ro híc súil ind ríg a topor Locha Dá Líg is í asibed sin dig la mnaí nÉtair hi tromdig. Is tría ág dossib in rí inna héonu di Thethbí Ocus báidfid a dá ech i llind Locha Dá Airbre Bíat imda coicthe ili tríat ág for Echaig Midi íaid togal for sídib Ocus cath for ilmilib. Is í ro loited is tír is í archosnai in rig is í Be Find fris dogair is í ar nÉtaín iar tain.

"Etain today is here thus at Sídhe Ban Find west of Albai among girl children at the border of Inbir Cíchmuini. It is she who cured the eye of the king from the spring of lake Dá Líg[14] it is she who was drunk in that drink of the woman Étair; a heavy drink. Because of her the king will attack[15] birds from Thethbí[16] and drown his two horses in the pool of lake Da Airbe Bíat[17] much war will be waged many hosts battling upon Echaig of Meath bringing destruction of Fairy mounds and battle of many thousands. It is she who will devastate the land, it is she that goes to the king, it is she Be Find,[18] she is called our Étaín now."

Etain indiu. .n. Dochúaid úadib in t-óclaech iar sain iocus ní fetatar can dodeochaid la cid iarom.

O ránic in Mac Óc do acallaim Midir ní fornic Fuamnaig ara chiund ocus asbert .i. Midir "fris bréc dorat in ben imond ocus día n-ecastar dí Etain do bith i nÉre. Ocus ragaid do denam uilc fria."

"Domuiniur is dóig bid fir" ol Mac Óc. "Atá Étaín ocom thigsi isin Bruig o chíanaib isin deilb hi tarfas uaitsiu. Ocus bes is cuice forobart in ben."

Etain at that time went from the young man and was different afterwards and they didn't know whence he came from or yet went afterwards.

When the Mac Óc reached Midir to address him without help he didn't find Fuamnacht and said, that is Midir [said], to him "The woman has deceived us and if she has learned that Etain was alive in Ireland. And she will have gone to perpetrate evil on her."

"I believe it is likely to be true" said Mac Óc. "Étaín has been at my home at the Brug for a time in that form displayed since going from you. And it may be towards her the woman is rushing."

Dotháet Mac Óc día thig fora chulu co farnic a gríanán nglainidi cen Etaín and. Immasoí in Mac nÓc for slict Fuamnaige co tarraid for Óenuch Bodbgnai oc tig Bresail Etarláin in drúad. Fosnopair in Mac Óc ocus benaid a cend di & dobert lais a cend sin co rrabi for brú in Broga. Acht chena iss ed islicht i nn-inud aile conid la Manandán ro marbait a ndís .i. Fuamnach ocus Midir i mBri Léith día n-ébrad.

Mac Óc returned back to the house and found her crystal bower without Etaín there. The Mac nÓc turned around on the trail of Fuamnacht and overtook her at Óenuch Bodbgnai[19] at the house of Bresail Etarláin the druid. The Mac Óc attacked her and he struck her head off so that he brought her head then with him to the Brú in Broga. But moreover, however, common people say in other versions it was Manannán who killed the two that is Fuamnach and Midir in Bri Léith. Some say:

Fúamnach báeth bá ben Midir Sigmall is brí co mbilib i mBrí Léith ba láthar lan ro loiscthe la Manandán.

"Reckless Fúamnach was the wife of Midir, Sigmall was a hill of ancient trees, in Brí Léith was their full power burnt by Manannán."

This is where the available Irish text ends. In the story the strange rider's prediction comes to pass: Etain marries the king of Ireland. Midir finds her in her new form and wins a forfeit from the king – he claims a single kiss from Etain. When the two kiss she remembers her former life and Midir turns the two into swans who fly away. The king pursues them, fighting to get back his wife. Finally, Midir makes 50 women look like Etain and tells the king he can keep her if he chooses the real one; instead the king mistakenly chooses his own daughter, who he fathers a daughter on. Etain and Midir return to the Sidhe together.

Chapter 2

The Ulster Cycle

Possibly the most well-known of the Irish mythic material is the Ulster Cycle which includes the Táin Bó Cúailgne, the cattle raid of Cooley, as well as various pre-tales and follow up stories centred on Cu Chulainn and the Ulster warriors more generally. It is far beyond the scope of this humble book to include the entire Ulster cycle of course but this chapter encompasses all of the pieces from that cycle that I have translated so far, many of which feature the Aos Sidhe or figures like the Morrigan.

De Chophur in Da Muccida
The Struggle of the Two Swineherds

In my opinion one of the most essential pre-tales, this explains the true nature of the two famous bulls of the Táin Bó Cúailgne and why they have such animosity for each other. The Irish text is from Stokes & Windsch's 1880 article in Irische Texte mit Übersetzugen und Wörterbuch.

Ceist cid dia dá Cophur na Muccide. Ni handsa. .i. muccaid Ochaill Oichni. & muccaid Boidb rig síde Muman. alaile rí síde Connacht. Síd mBoidb iss ed Síd ar Femun. Sid nOchaill iss ed Síd Cruachan. Ro boí dí cairddes eter ríg side Muman. & ríg side Connacht. Ro batar dano da muccaid ocaib .i. Friuch & Rucht a n-anmand .i. Friuch muccaid Boidb. Rucht muccaid Ochaill. Ro boí dano carddess eturrusaide .i. suithe ngentlechta la cechtar de. & nos delbtais in cech richt. amal no bíth Mongán mac Fiachna.

What caused the struggle of the two swineherds? Not difficult. That is the swineherd of Ochaill Oichni and the swineherd of Bodb king of the sídhe of Munster, the other the king of the sídhe of Connacht. The sídhe of Bodb that is the sídhe at Femun. The sídhe of Ochaill that is the sídhe of Cruachan. There was friendship between the king of the sídhe of Munster. and the king of the sidhe of Connacht. There were therefore two swineherds with them that is Friuch and Rucht where their names. That is Friuch was the swineherd of Bodb. Rucht the swineherd of Ochaill. There was also friendship between them that is both having pagan knowledge between them and had the habit of taking on many forms, like Mongán mac Fiachna would.

Ba he carddes na da muccaidse .i. In tan ba mess la Mumnechu. Do theiged in muccaid atúaid cona muccaib caelaib fadess. In tan ba mess danoatúaid. no theiged in muccaid andess fathúaith. Consoíter debuid eturru. Asbertis Connachta ba mó cumachta a mmuccida. Asbertis Mumnig dano ba mó cumachta a mmuccida.

This was the friendship of the two swineherds that is when there were masts in Munster the swineherd came from the north with his thin pigs to the south. When the masts were in the north the swineherd from the south went north. Strife was stirred up between them. The people of Connacht said the power of their swineherd was greater. The people of Munster however said that the power of their swineherd was greater.

Bliadain and dano mess mór la Mumnechu & dolluid in muccaid atúaid fadess cona muccaib leis. Feraid a cheile failte ris.

"Consaíter etrunni mad tú" ol se. "Asberat ind firseo is mó do chumachtasu indausa."

"Ni lugu ém" ol muccaid Ochaill.

"Bieid ní i fessamar ón" ol muccaid Boidb. "Dogensa urgaire do muccsu connápat metha ce beit for mess."

One year there the masts were great in Munster and the swineherd from the north came south with his swine. He supplied his fellow a welcoming bit of news.

"They are trying to stir us up" said he. "They say the strength and greater power is yours."

"It is not less" said Ochaill's swineherd.

"There is a way to know this" said Bodb's swineherd. "I will restrain your swine with a harbored wasting despite the mast, and without wasting on my own pigs."

Ocus bat metha mo mucca féin. Ocus immarránic anísin iarum. Téit muccaid Ochaill dia thaig iarum cona muccaib caelaib leis. iss infechtain rosiachtatar less ar throgi. Con- tibther immiseom o ránic a thír.

"Olc húar lodsai" ol cach fris. "Is mó cumachta do cheili andaí"

"Ni bá anísin" ol sesseom. "Biaid mess lenni atherruch & dogensa in cless cetna risseom. & immarranic son dano iarum."

And so it went with them afterwards. The swineherd of Ochaill went home after with his thin pigs, who scarcely could follow to the courtyard because of their wretchedness. They smiled on him when he arrived back in his land.

"You went at an evil hour" they all said to him. "The greater power is with your fellow."

"This is not good," said he. "The mast will be with us again and I will perform the same feat. And it will follow thus with him after."

Téit muccaid Boidb fathúaid a dochumsom día bliadna cona muccaib caelaib leiss i tíre Connacht. & dogeni muccaid Ochaill a cetna fria muccasom coro serggsat. Co n-erbairt cách ba cumma a cumachtu dib linaib. Luid muccaid Boidb atúaid cona muccaib caelaib leiss. Gataid

Bodb a muccaidecht n-airi. Gatar dano a muccaidecht arin fer atúaith. Dí bliadain lána dóib iar sin i ndelbaib senén.

The swineherd of Bodb went back north after a year of his power with his thin pigs with him in the land of Connacht. And it was the same as it had first been with the swineherd of Ochaill's pigs with wasting. So people said the power was equal power with them. The swineherd of Bodb came back from the north with his thin pigs with him. Bodb took away his office of swineherd, of guarding. Taken away as well was the office of swineherd regarding the man in the north. Two whole years they are after that in different shapes.

Indala bliadain túaid la Connachta for Dún Chruachan in bliadain aile dóib oc Síd ar Femun. Condrancatar fir Muman i n-oendáil laa n-óen and. "Ní bec a ndeilm dogniat ind eoin arfar mbelaib." ol eat. "bliadain lán o tát ocond imchiradsa & ocund ábairtse cosindiu."

One year north in Connacht at the fort of Cruachan the other year they are at the Sídhe al Femun.

The men of Munster came together in a gathering on a certain day there.

"Not small the noise the birds are making with their mouths." they said. "a whole year of them raising outrage and raising battle-cries until today."

Tan iarum batar forsna briathraibse co n-accatar rechtaire Ochaill chuccu issin telaig. Fuidell mac Fiadmire a ainmside. ferthair failte friss. "Is mór a ndeilm dogniat ind eóin arbar mbelaib. Indar lat batir hé da én batar ocund atuaith innuraid."

Then after they were speaking they saw the steward of Ochaill coming to them on the mound. His name was Fuidell mac Fiadmire. They welcomed him. "It is a great din the birds are making with their mouths. You would think these were the two birds that were stirring up in the north last year."

Ocus iss ed dano dogníside co cend mbliadna a cetna. Co n-accat ní iar suidiu batar delba doíne. in da sinén hísin. Ataciat iar suidiu batir é a ndá muccid. Ferait failti friu.

And it was thus they had been in conflict the first year. Then they saw after that they were in the form of people, the two who had been birds. They could see then the two swineherds. They welcomed them.

"Ni fíu falti frinn" or muccaid Boidb "biaid mór colla cóem ocus mór núall diar n-ág ar ndís."

"Cichib róer" ol Bodb.

"It is not fitting to welcome us," said the swineherd of Bodb "There will be great destruction of fair men.and great shouting arising from the battle of this pair."

"What causes this?" said Bodb

"Nin foruireth na mmaith" ol se. "O lodmarni uaibse ol se dib línaib dí blíadain lána cossindiu. Ataam i ndelbaib én. Adchondarcfarsi a ndoringensamni arbar mbelaib Bliadain lán dún i Cruachnaib ocund urdsin. Bliadain aile oc Sid ar Femun. Co n-faccatar ind fir atúaid & indess ar cumachta díb línaib. Regmai dano ifechtsa i ndelba míl uisci & bemmit fo murib co cend dá bliadna aile. Documlat uadib iar sin cechtar n-aí a leth. Luid indala n-aí i Sinnaind luid alaile i sSiúir."

"We bring about nothing good," said he. "O since we have gone from you" said he "We have been two full years until today in the shape of birds. You have witnessed our actions. A full year at the fort of Cruachan raising a cry. The other year at Sid ar Femun. Both the men of the north and south have seen the power of each of us. We will go thus now in the shape of water animals and be under the sea with this skin for two more years. We will set out from you after that each on his own way. One of the two to go to the Shannon the other to go to the Suir."

Batir iar sin da bliadain lana fon uisci. Bliadain lán atchitís i sSiúir ic immithi. In bliadain aile dano atchitis i sSinaind. Batar dano da n-oss. & teclamad cechtar n-aí osséti co ndenad damlíg do mennut a cheile. Batir da fennid & imgonad cechtar de a chéle. Batir da siabuir & fobuthad cechtar de a chéile. Batir da draic túarcad cechtar de snechta for tír a cheili.

They were after that two full years in the water. A full year biting and devouring one another in the Suir. The other year therefore biting each other in the Shannon. They were moreover two deer and gathered together one of the two the other's herd with violent damage to the abode of his fellow. They were two warriors and each struck at his fellow. They were phantoms and each frightened his fellow. They were two dragons each smiting with snow the land of his fellow.

Dofuittet díb línaib assind aér comtar di dorbbi. Teit indala n-aí i topur Glaisse Cruind i Cualngiu. conda essib bó Dáiri meic Fiachnai. & teit alaile i n-Uarán nGarad la Connachta conda ib bó Medba & Ailella conid díb ro chinset in da tharb. in Finnbennach Aí & in Dub Cualngi. Rúcht & Runce. imtar dá muccid. Ingen & Eitte imdar da sinén. Bled & Blod imtar da míl fo murib. Rind & Faebur imtar da fénnid. Scáth & Scíath imtar dí siabair. Crunniuc & Tuinniuc imdar dí dorbbai. Finnbend Aí & in Dond Cualngi a n-anmand in tan batar da tharb.

They dropped out of the air becoming small insects. One went in the well of Glaisse Cruind in Cualngi and was drunk by a cow of Dáiri meic Fiachnai. And the other went to Uarán nGarad of Connacht and was drunk by a cow of Medb and Ailill so that the two bulls were born from them. The White-horned of Aí and the

Black of Cualngi. Rúcht[20] and Runce where the two swineherds. Ingen[21] and Eitte[22] were the two birds. Bled[23] and Blod[24] were the two animals under water. Rind[25] and Faebur[26] were the two warriors. Scáth[27] and Scíath[28] were the two phantoms. Crunniuc and Tuinniuc were the two insects. Finnbend Aí[29] and the Donn Cualngi[30] the names that were on the two bulls.

Verba Scaithage
Scathach's Words

Cu Chulainn had gone to the mysterious warrior woman Scathach for training, as part of his efforts to woo Emir. When his training was finished Scathach had these words for him, a prophecy of his future in the form of a poem. The Irish text was accessed on a public website, as a reprint of an article, which can be found under the poem's title in the bibliography.

Incipiunt uerba Scathaige fri Con Culainn oc scarad doib isna rannuib tair. Ro scaith do Choin Culainn lanfogluim in milti la Scaithaigh. Do aurchechain Scathach do iarum ind ni arad m-biad, con-eipirt friss tria imbass for ossna.

Here start the words between Scathach and Cu Chulainn as they parted in the eastern area. This occured after Cu Chulainn completed his military training with Scathach. Scathach foretold to him then the things to happen in his life, speaking through imbas forosna

Imbe eir hengaile
arat-ossa ollgabud
huatha fri heit n-imlebair .i. tain bo Cuailgne

When arises the bird-of-valor
Vast-danger awaits you
Few against a great herd, that is the Cattle Raid of Cooley

Cotat curaith ciallfaithir
fortat braigait bibsatur
bied do chailcc culbeimnech

Harsh against your senses
Striking necks to breaking
Your [sling] stones will be buffeting

cruoch fri srut Setanta .i. proprium nomen do Choin Culainn.
Tithis fithog foibharamnus
fethal feula fedchlessaib

Gory against Setanta's stream, that is your proper name Cu Chulainnn.
Swearing oaths stripping young trees
Halidom of bloody weapons-feats

fearba do Breig m-braitfiter
braighit di thuaith tithsithir
tren cithach coictigis

Cows to Breig [Meath] will be raided away
Your people's captives will be slain
Strong blows for a fortnight

cichis do buar m-belata
ba hoín fri slog sirdochrae
silfis de fhuil flandtedman

Your cattle will go on the crossroads
You alone against a marauding host
Showers of blood, deadly-blood-red

fernaib ilib idlochtaib
cuan dia-lilis loscandaib
lin do-fedat ildamaib

On the shields of many warriors
A band who clings like vermin
A multitude they will lead many cattle

ilar fuili firfith-
for Coin Culainn cen colainn
Ceisfe alag n-enchride

An abundance of deep wounds
On your flesh Cu Chulainnn
You will suffer a wound of heart-blemishing

al de dalaib dedairbe
didirn brodircc brisfithir
bruthaich fri toinn trechtaide

Beyond the second partition of it
Therefore urging ravaging battle-breaking
Furious against a thundering wave

frissin m-belend m-bandernech
belenn di chet clesamnach
cichet biet banchuire

Against a hero of iron-blows
A hero of many weapon-feats
A women-troop will beat their breasts

baiti Medb sceo Aillellai
arat-osa ollgabadh otharlighi.
Ucht fri h-echtga irgairgi

Overwhelming Medb and Ailill
Healing in a sickbed awaits you.
A face against long-fierce slaughter

at-chiu firfeith Finnbennach Aei
fri Donn Cuailngi ardburach & cetera.

I see well-muscled Finnbennach Ai
Against the Donn of Cooley loud bellowing and so on.

Excerpt from Bricrui's Feast: The Awarding of the Hero's Portion

I wanted to include this because it has the fascinating phrase 'Tong a toing mo tuath' – "I swear the oath of my people" which appears across the stories and seems to be a common oath taking motif. It is a piece of a wider tale about three Ulster warriors fighting over who is the greatest champion among them and therefore entitled to the hero's portion at feasts. Because Conchobar didn't want to make the decision and risk the wrath of the other two he sent all three to Medb and Ailill, effectively putting them on the spot to make the decision. Medb eventually does so, after a series of trials not included here, but rather than announcing it and angering them herself she sends them all back to Ulster, each with a cup of different value. Only when they get back and publicly compare cups do they realize who has been named the champion.

The Irish text was transcribed from the 1884 Irische Texte mit Übersetzugen und Wörterbuch

---

Luid iarom Ailill ina arucul folet fri scrutuin a mbrethaigthi & domber a druimm fri fraigid & ni ba saim a menma & ba difficulty les an dail donfáinec & ni rochodail & ni roloingti co cend tri laa & teora n-oidqi, conid ann ismbert Medb: 'Is milaechda' 'no tái', ol si.

[gap]

Ailill went afterwards [to his] private apartments to ponder his judgement and with his back against the interior wall and had no rest in his mind and was in difficulty seeking relief to this problem and without sleep and without eating to the end of three days and three nights, and thereafter spoke Medb: "martial prowess" "or a cup, " she said.

[gap:]

Dotrae suas lasodain an cuach ndercoir & en do liic logmair for a lár & cutraime hi sula di draccain, dotnacatar Ulaid uili im Concubar mac Nessa. "Is me ierom dligius a curadmir, mina brister fior fer form."

"Cotmidium uili", ol Concubar & Fercus & ol maithi Ulad uili, "is let an curadmir a brith n-Ailellai."

He [Cu Chulainn] rose up then with the pure-gold cup and birds of precious stones on the middle and two dragon-stones the size of his eyes, he said to all the men of Ulster with Conchubar mac Nessa, "Mine then by right the warrior's portion, unless they break fair play."

"To you we all judge it", said Conchubar and Fergus and said the good men of Ulster, "and the warrior's portion has been decided by Allil."

'Tong a toing mo tuath', or Loegairi Buadach & ol Connall, 'ni cuach cin crec dit an cuach tucuis. In rusboi di hsetaibh & di moinibh it hseulba, tucuis airi di Ailill & Meidb, ar na ructha dou bhag it cend, na tarta in curadmir di neoch aili ar do bheluib.'

'Tong a toing mo tuath', or Connall, 'ni ba lat, & ni ba breth an breth donucad ann, & ni berai an curadmir.'

"I swear the oath of my people," said Loegairi Buadach and said Connall, "any cup you have is a plunder taken not the cup given away. You have been bestowed it [because] from your treasure and possessions, you have given to Ailill and Medb, so that the giving of this declaration is the result, the warriors portion yours alone."

"I swear the oath of my people", said Connall, "this thing will not stand, and it is no justice the judgement given there, and any judgement of the warriors portion."

Táin Bó Regamna
The Cattle Raid of Regamna

My favourite pre-tale and another extremely essential story in understanding the wider reason that the Táin Bó Cuiliagne occurred this Táin is the story of Cu Chulainn and his charioteer Laeg meeting a myseterious couple driving a cow out of Ulster which culminates in a prediction of the Táin Bó Cuiliagne and promises by the Morrigan to attack Cu Chulainn. The promises to attack Cu Chulainn are an essential aspect of both this story and the Táin Bó Cúailgne, and establishes the animosity between the two. The story dates to the 9th century but like much of the material here the Irish used is from Egerton 1782, which was written in the 16th century. The Irish text is taken from Irish from Stokes, W., (1884). Irische Texte mit Übersetzugen und Wörterbuch

---

A mbuí Cú Chuluinn i nDún Imrid gu gcúala ní an géim. Co ndíuchrustar triana chotlad conid corustar asa imda go riacht ind aridin ina suidiu for lár. Íar sin immach do suidiu ar les. Cu mbu hí a ben bertho a étach ocus a armb ina diaig. Co n-facco ní Láeg aro chinn ina charpat inneltai oc Ferta Læig intúaig.

When Cu Chulainn was in Dun Imrid he heard something; it was the roaring of cattle. So that he woke up and was thrown out of bed and reached the bench that was sitting on the floor. After that he went outside into the yard. And it was his wife, following behind him, who brought his clothing and his armor. And he saw something in front of him, Laeg in his chariot, harnessed at Ferta Laeg in the north.

'Cid dot-ugai?' ol Cú Chuluinn fri Lóeg.
'Géim ro-chúalai issin maigh', ol Lóeg.
'Cid leth?' ol Cú Chuluinn.
'Aníarthúaig amne', ol Lóeg.
'Ina ndiaig', ol Cú Chuluinn.

"What brings you?" said Cu Chulainn to Laeg.
"The roaring of cattle that I heard in the field," said Laeg.
"What direction?" said Cu Chulainn.
"In the north-west, thus," said Laeg.
"Follow on then," said Cu Chulainn.

Tíaguit ass íarum gu hÁth da Ferta. In tan mbátar ann íarum gu gcúalatar culguiri in charpuit hi toíb Grellchui Culguiri. Tíaguit fóe co n-faccatar ní in carpat ara cinn no reimib. Óenech derg foa ocus óenchoss fo suidiu ocus síthbe in charpuit sethnu ind eich co ndechuid geinn trít fri fosad a étain anair. Bean derg hissin charpat ocus bratt derg impi ocus di braí dergai lé ocus a brat eter di feirt in charpuit síar co sliged lár ina diaig ocus fer mór hi comuir in charpuit. Fúan forbbthai imme ocus gaballorg finnchuill fria aiss og immáin na bó.

After this they went out to Ath de Ferta. After, while they were there, they heard a noise of the chariot in the side of Grellach Culgairi. They went down and saw a chariot before them. One red horse with a single leg was pulling it, and the shaft of the chariot went through the horse to the front of its forehead. A red-haired woman with red eyebrows was in the chariot with a red cloak around her shoulders; the cloak hung down at the back of the chariot and dragged on the ground behind her. There was a big man in front of the chariot wearing a tunic carrying a forked white hazel stick that he used to drive the cow.

'Ní fóelid in bó lib oga himmuáin', ol Cú Chuluinn.

'Ní dír duit éim a hetercert na bó so', ol in ben. 'Ní bó charat na choigcéliu duit.'

'Is dír dam-so éim baí hUlad huili', ol Cú Chuluinn.

'Eter-certar so in ba, a Chú', ol in ben.

"The cow is not pleased with her driving," said Cu Chulainn.

"Indeed, it is not necessary to you to judge this cow," said the woman. "It is not a friend's nor a companion's cow to you."

"Indeed, the cows of all the Ulstermen are necessary to me," said Cu Chulainn

"You decide much, oh, Cu Chulainn," said the woman.

'Ced arndid i in ben atum-gládathar?' ol Cú Chuluinn. 'Cid nach é in fer atom-gládathar?'

'In fer sin at-gládaigther-su', ol in ben.

'Ia', ol Cú Chuluinn, 'ol is tusso ara-labrathar.'

'hÚargóeth sceo lúachuir sgeo. . .ainm in fir sin', olsí.

'Amae, is amru fot in anmu', ol Cú Chului nn. 'Ba tusa trá atom glátathar in fecht so ol nim acalladar in fer. Cía do chomainm-siu féin?' ol Cú Chuluinn.

"Why is it that the woman speaks to me?" said Cu Chulainn. "Why not him, the man, who speaks to me?"

"It's not the man that you shouted to", said the woman.

"Ha!", said Cu Chulainn, "Speak and you speak in his voice."

"Cold wind-conflict-brightness-strife is his name" she said

"Indeed, that name is wonderful throughout", said Cu Chulainn. "Then you are bound to speaking the course of this conversation for the man. What do you name yourself?" said Cu Chulainn.

'Ní ansa. In ben sin at-gládaither-su', ol in fer, 'fóebar beo béoil, coim diúir, foltt sgeanb, gairitt sgeo úath hí a hainm', olse.

'Meraigi do-gníth-siu dim-so', ol Cú Chuluinn, 'fon innus sin.'

"Not difficult. The woman who you are speaking to," said the man, "is Keen edged-small lipped-plain cloaked-hair-sharp shouting-fierceness-a phantom."

"You give me an idiot's counsel,"[31] said Cu Chulainn, "based in this."

Lingid Cú Chuluinn la soduin issin charpat ocus fo-rrumai a da chois fora dib glúinib-siu ocus a chleitíni fora mullach.

'Na himbir imrinniu éim formb', ol Cú Chuluinn.

'Scuith dim didiu', olsi.

Cu Chulainn jumped beside her in the chariot and set his two feet on her knees and his dart[32] against the crown of her head."Who puts this point indeed?" said Cu Chulainn.

"A small something then", said she.

'Am bancháinti-siu ém', olsí, 'ocus is ó Dáiriu mac Fiachno a cCúailgniu tuccus in mbuin si a ndúais n-airchetail.'

'Cluinium th'airchetal didiu', ol Cú Chuluinn.

'Scuith dim nammá', ol in ben. 'Ní ferdo duitt amin na chrothai húas mo chinn', olsí.

Tét didiu Cú Chuluinn íarum co mbuí eter di feirt in charpuit.

"I am a woman satirist indeed", said she, "and it is from Dáire mac Fiachnai of Cuilgne that I bring the cow; she is a poet's reward for a poem"'

"I'll hear the poem then", said Cu Chulainn.

"A small something only", said the woman. "Not manly to you thus while brandishing over my head", said she.

Then after Cu Chulainn went so that he was between the two poles of the chariot.

Gaibid-se in laíd si: Doermais nomgaib gaib eti eblatar tairichta muirtemniu morochrat romlec dianedim fiach amainsi nachach toarbair adomling airddhe oenmairb maige sainb croí chengach cocbith mestin- glinne let leiss finn frithoiss dobeoib brectith reth tuasailg osdum arai airdd cechlastair cuailngne achuchuluinn...

She gave this poem:[33] "Low-born-foundation you grab,
Take a herd driven,
Eastward-blown Muirrthemne,
Great misery, chief stone, hurrier,
Raven fierce but not
Bringing great floods
Peak of fame unique death
Plain of Sainb heart, every head
World-warring judgment
Half a glen severed
Bright wild place, your life
Deceitful arrival runs
Over poet's-demands
Over mound's messenger
Your direction, every burning
Cuailigne, oh Cu Chulainnn..."

Fo-ceird Cú Chuluinn bedg ina charpat feissin íarum. Naicc ní i nneoch íarum in mnaí nach in carpat nach in n-ech nach in fer nach in mbuin ocus co n-faco-sium íarum ba hén-si dub forsin chroíb ina farrud.

'Doltach ben atat-chomnaic', ol Cú Chuluinn.

'Is Dollud dono bias forsinn greallaig si co bráth', ol in ben. Grellach Dolluid íarum a hainm ó hoin ille.

Cu Chulainn sprang onto his own chariot after that. Then nothing was there of all of them not the woman, not the chariot, not the horse, not the man, not the cow and he saw that she was a black bird on a branch near him.

"A hurtful woman you are," said Cu Chulainn.

"It is Dollud [distress] then that will be on this bog until Doomsday," said the woman. Bog of Distress was its name from that time afterwards.

'Ochti ro-feisind bed tú ní samluid no-scarfamais', ol Cú Chuluinn.

'Cid donrignis', olsí, 'bieith olec de.'

'Ni chumgai olc dam', ol Cú Chuluinn.

'Cumgaim écin', olsin ben. 'Is oc do ditin do báis-siu atáu-so ocus bia', ollsí.

"If only I had known it was you," said Cu Chulainn, "not this way would we have separated."

"Whatever you would have done," said she, "misfortune would result from it."

"You cannot bring misfortune to me," said Cu Chulainn.

"I am able indeed," said the woman; "It is bringing about your death I am and shall be,"[34] said she.

'Do-ucus-sa in mboin si éim', olsí, 'a síd Crúachan condo rodart in Donn Cúailgni lem .i. tarb Dáre maic Fiachnui ocus is é aret bia-so i mbetho gu rab dartaid in lóeg fil ina bruinn ina bó so ocus is hé consaídfe Táin Bé Cúailgni.'

"I brought this cow then," she said, "from the fairy mound of Cruachan so that she was mounted by the Brown Bull of Cuilgne by me, that is the bull of Daire mac Fiachnai. And it is that interval you will be in life, until the calf in the womb of this cow is a young bull, and it is this that stirs up the cattle raid of Cuilgne."

'Bíam airdirciu-sa di din Táin hí sin', ol Cú Chuluinn.

''Géna a n-ánrado.
Brisfe a mérchatho.

Bia tigba na Táno.''

"I will be renowned through this aforementioned cattle raid," said Cu Chulainn.
"I will kill their champions.
Defeat their big battles.
I will survive the cattle raid."

'Cinnus con-igfa-sa anní sin', ol in ben. 'Ar in tain no-mbia-sa oc comrac fri fer comthrén comchroda comchliss comfobaith coméscaith comchiníuil comgaiscid comméti friut .i. bam esccung-so ocus fo-chichiur curu immot chossa issinn áth gu mba héccomlunn mór.'

"How will you do this aforementioned?" said the woman. "For at the time of your combat with a man of similar strength, similar form, similar skill, similar quickness, similar alertness, similar tribe, similar weapons, similar greatness, against you I will be an eel throwing twists about your feet in the ford until it will be greatly unfair odds."

'For-tonga do día tuingthe Ulaid', ol Cú Chuluinn, 'fortat-naesab su fri glaisslecta ind átho ocus nicot bia ícc húaim-siu de gu bráth manim derguis-so.'

'Bia sod-sa dono glass duit-si', olsí, 'ocus géba bréit dot dóidind deiss conicci do rigid clí.'

"I swear to a God Ulstermen swear to," said Cu Chulainn, "I will kick you against blue-grey[35] stones of the ford and there will be no cure for you from me[36] for it until Doomsday if you don't ask my forgiveness."

"I will be a blue-grey[37] wolf-bitch then against you," she said. "And I will take a strip from your wrist on the right up to your forearm on the left."

'Tongu-sa do día tuingti hUlaid', ol Cú Chuluinn, 'not-benabsi secham gom chletíne gu mbeba do súil it chinn ocus nocot bia ícc húaim-siu de go bráth manim dergais-si.'

'Biam samuiscc-siu finn áuoderg dono', olsissiu, 'ocus do-rag issinn linn hi fail inn áthu in n-atan ro-mbia-so oc comrucc fri fer buss choimchliss duitt ocus cét noud finn n-óbrecc imm diaig ocus membuis inn ét huili im diaig-siu issin n-áth ocus con-bibustar fír fer fort-so a llaa sin ocus géttair do chenn ditt issinn áth sin.'

"I swear to a God Ulstermen swear to," said Cu Chulainn,"I will wound you myself with my dart until your eye bursts in your head and there will be no cure for you from me for it until Doomsday if you don't ask my forgiveness."

"I will be a red-eared white heifer then," said she, "and I will come in the water in a place of the ford another time you will be at combat with a man as skilled as you and a hundred red-eared white cows after me; all the cows behind me will burst into the ford and violate fair combat[38] against you. And your head will be taken away off you in that very ford."

'Tungu et reliqua, fo-chichiur-sa hurchur asmo thábaill fortt sa co memba do gerr gara foat ocus nico mbia ícc húaim-si de co bráth manim dergais-si ocus nicom géntar-so a llá sin etir', ol Cú Chuluinn.

Scarsait íar sin ocus luid Cú Chuluinn for cúlo dorithisiu do Dún Imrith ocus luithi in Morrígan cona buin hi síd Crúachan la Connachta.

"I will swear by others, I will throw a cast out of my sling at you and with it break the lower part of your leg shortly and by no means will there be a cure for you from me for it until Doomsday if you don't ask my forgiveness and that will not be done any day at all', said Cu Chulainn.

They separated and Cu Chulainn went back along his course to Dún Imrith and the Morrigan went with the cow to the fairy hill of Cruachan in Connacht.

The Morrigan's Satire Poem

I thought it would be interesting to show you the differences between the two versions of the Morrigan's satire poem which appear in different versions of the *Táin Bó Regamna*. I'll give the Yellow Book of Lecan version first followed by the von Egerton version, both found in Irish in the Irische Texte mit Übersetzugen und Wörterbuch:

Doernais namgaib
Gaib eiti ablatutar
ie n Muirrthemne
(daruber .i. arg mag Murthemne).
Moracrat romleic diamaigi
fiachanma amanse
nach cach do arbiur
adomlig.
Ardbae aen marb
maigi Sainb (daruber .i. Ai)
Cerda croichengach
cochbith metsin glinni
lat les find fir itho is de
buaib brethai treth
tuasailc os do marai
airdde cechlastar
Cnailngi a Cuculainn fri
burach mbuaid ar
cuailgi a Cuchulainn cair.
Buidi ben basa claen
cuil arm deisi ar saegal
dian taith .i. cluas armgreta.

Slave-bound you grab
Take a herd driven
Gifts of Muirrthemne
(that is noble plain of Muirrthemne)
Great misery, chief stone, mighty lamentation,
Fierce ravens
Not each to you brings
Great fearsome glory.
High-profit a unique death
the plain of Sainb (that is Ai)
Skilled each-skin
World-warring judgment glens
Half severed, bright men hunger and you
arrogant decide a herd
Above demands and your existence
Your direction, every burning
Cuiligne, oh Cu Chulainn, towards
Furious victory from
Cuiligne, oh guilty Cu Chulainn.
Gratitude a woman unjust death
Violating weapon, hosts against a lifetime
True binding, that is here weapons-strikes

The alternate von Egerton version is:
Doermais nomgaib
gaib eti eblatar
tairichta muirtemniu
morochrat romlec dianedim
fiach amainsi nachach
toarbair adomling
airddhe oenmairb
maige sainb croí chengach
cocbith mestin-

glinne let leiss
finn frithoiss dobeoib
brectith reth
tuasailg osdum arai
airdd cechlastair
cuailngne achuchuluinn.

"Low-born-foundation you grab,
Take a herd driven,
Eastward-blown Muirrthemne,
Great misery, chief stone, hurrier,
Raven fierce but not
Bringing great floods
Peak of fame unique death
Plain of Sainb heart, every head
World-warring judgment
Half a glen severed
Bright wild place, your life
Deceitful arrival runs
Over poet's-demands
Over mound's messenger
Your direction, every burning
Cuilnge, oh Cu Chulain..."

Descriptions of Fidelm

These are two consecutive passages which are descriptions from different recensions of the *Táin Bó Cuiliagne* of Medb's encounter with a fairy woman and prophetess named Fidelm.

Impáis in t-ara in carpat ocus dothaét Medb for cúlu, co n-accai ní rap ingnad lé, .i. in n-aenmnái for fertais in charpait na farrad ina dochum. Is amlaid bói ind ingen: ic figi corrthairi ocus claideb findruini ina láim deiss cona secht n-aslib do dergór ina dessaib; bratt ballabrecc uani impi; bretnas torrach trencend sin brutt osa brunni; gnúis chorcra chrumainech lé; rosc glass gairectach le; beóil derga thanaide; dét niamda nemanda, andar let batar frossa findnémand erctais ina cend; cosmail do nuapartaing a beóil; binnidir téta mendchrot aca seinm allámaib sirshúad bindfogur a gotha ocus a cáinurlabra; gilidir snechta sniged fri oenaidchi taidlech a cniss ocus a colla sech a timthach sechtair; traigthi seta sithgela, ingni corcra córi cruindgéra lé; folt findbudi fata forórda furri; teora trillsi da fult imma cend, trilis aile co m-benad foscad fri colptha.

Irische Texte Mit Ubersetzungen, Windisch (1905.)

"The charioteer turned the chariot and suddenly at Medb's back, she saw something, a person unusual to her, that is the single girl at a shaft of the chariot beside the company. And thus is the girl: besides weaving fringe and a sword of fine brass in her right hand, seven sword-ornaments of red-gold well arranged on it; a speckled-spotted green cloak on her; a brooch rounded, strong-covered there on her cloak and chest; a face red , rich-blooded with her; eyes green and laughing with her; a subtle red mouth; brilliant pearl-like teeth, you would think they were white-pearls showering abundantly from her head; similar to fresh scarlet were her lips; melodious strings of a lyre being played by a master, long lasting, sweet-sounding her voice and her enchanting speech; bright as falling snow from a single night was her shining skin and her body that was beyond her garment; feet slender long and fair, nails dark red, well-proportioned, round and neat with her; hair light-yellow , long, and golden on her; three plaits of hair on her head, another plait with a shadow reaching to her calf."

Alternately from another recension:

'In tan didiu dosoí an t-ara forsin carpat ocus lotair do thecht ass co n-accatár in n-ingin macdacht remib. Folt buidi furri. Bratt brecc impe, delg n-óir and. Léine chulpatach co n-derggintslaid impe. Dá assa co foraib óir impu. Agad fochóel forlethan. Dí broí duba dorchaidi. Abrait duib dáin co m-bentaís foscod i m-medón a dá grúaide. Indar latt ropo di partaing imdéntai a beóil. Indar lat ba fross do némannaib boí inna bélaib .i. a fíaclai. Teóra trillsi fuirri .i. dí thriliss immo cend súas, trilis tara h-aiss síar co m-benad a dá colptha inna díaid. Claideb corthaire do findruine inna láim, esnaid óir and. Trí meic imlisse cechtar a dá súla. Gaisced lasin n-ingin & dá ech duba foa carput.'

Táin Bó Cúailnge, Recension 1, Lebor na hUidre,

Then when the charioteer turns the chariot back and had gone, they saw the girl of marriageable age before them. Yellow hair on her. A speckled cloak on her, red-gold there. A hooded tunic with red-embroidery about her. Two shoes with gold on them. Her face slender below, broad above. Two heavy dark black eyelashes, delicate they look, which cast a shadow in the middle of her two cheeks. You would think fresh crimson adorns her mouth. You would think there were pearls there behind her lips, that is her teeth. Three plaits of hair with her that is two plaits about her head upwards, a plait covering her back down shadowing her calves to the end. A weaving beam of fine-brass in her right hand, inset with gold. Three pupils in each of her two eyes. Weapons with the girl and two black horses under her chariot.

Aided Óenfir Aífe
The Death Of Aife's Only Son

One of the most tragic tales in the Ulster Cycle may be the story of Cu Chulainn's son Conla, who is killed by his father after refusing to break several geasa, or prohibitions, that his father himself put on the boy. The Irish text is taken from from

Meyer;s 1904 'The Death of Conla from the Yellow Book of Lecan, 214a in Eriu 1

Cía fochann araro marb Cú Chulainn a mac? Ní hansae. Luid Cú Chulainn do forcetul gaiscid la Scáthaig n-Úanaind ingin Airdgeme i l-Letha co ndergéni súithi cles lea & luid Aífe ingen Airdgeme cuici & ba torrach forácaib & asbert fria no bérad mac.

What was the cause of the death of Cú Chulainn's son? Not difficult.

Cú Chulainn went for weapons instruction to Scáthach the Foam-white daughter of Airdgeme in Letha to gain mastery of feats with her and he went to Aoífe daughter of Airdgeme and he left her pregnant and said she would bear a son.

"Bíd ind ordnasc n-órdae so acut", ol sé, "corop coimse don mac. In tan bas coimse dó, táet dom chuindchidsea i n-Ére & nacham berad óenfer dia chonair & nacha sloinded do óenfiur & ná fémded comlann óenfir."

"Take this thumb-ring of gold to hold", he said, "until it is fit for the boy. When it is fit, let him come to seek me in Ireland and not give way to a single man on the road and not declare himself to a single man and not refuse combat to a single man."

Doluid in mac dia secht mblíadan do chuindchid a athar. Is and bátar Ulaid i n-óendáil oc Trácht Éise ara chiund. Co n-accatar in mac cucu íarsind fairci & luingine chrédumai fo suidiu & rámada dí-órdai ina láim. Carn cloch aici isin luing. Dobered cloich ina chrandtabaill & dosléiced táthbéim forsna héonu, co ngaibed na hairberta díb, ot é beóa, conda léiced úad isind áer doridisi. Imfuirmed a charpatchles eter a dí láim, conná tairthed súil. No glésed a guth dóib, conda foilged indara fecht. Dosnúisced in fecht n-aile.

The son went one day seven years afterwards to seek his father. The men of Ulster were in a gathering at Trácht Éise. They saw a boy coming towards them on the ocean and a bronze boat under him and gold oars in his hands. A heap of stones was with him in the boat. He would put a stone in his staff-sling and make a powerful throw on the birds, with skill taking them down, and they alive, releasing them into the air afterwards. He performs his palate-feat between his two hands, without the eye catching it. Or he would perform his voice for them, and spring on them a second time. Then revived them the next time.

"Maith tra," ol Conchobar, "mairg thír i táet in gillae ucut", ol sé. "Matis fir móra na hindsi asa táet donístis, conmeltis ar grian, in tan is mac bec dogni in airbert ucut. eirged nech ara chend. Nacha telged i tir eter"

"Cía regas ar a chend?"

"Cía-pad cía" ol Conchobar, "acht Cobdere mac Echach?"

"Cía immaregad Condere?" ol cách.

"Ní hansea," ol Conchobar, "cid cíall ocus erlabrea immabera is Condere as chóir and."

"Regadsa ar a chend." ol Condere.

"Good though," said Conchobar, "Woe to the land that the youth comes to", he said. "If great men of his island come to us, they would grind us to gravel, when a little boy makes this effort there. Someone go to meet him. Let him go anyway to another in land."

"Who should go meet him?"

"Who else" said Conchobar, "but Condere son of Echach?"

"Why should Condere?" everyone said.

"Not difficult," said Conchobar, "If it is good sense and nobility that is with him then Condere should meet him there."

"I will go meet him." said Condere.

Luid Condere íarom & is and ro gab in mac tráig in tan sin. 'Is lóor dothéig, a macáin,' ol Condere, 'co fessamar cid no théig & can do chenél.'

'Ním sloindim do óenfiur,' ol in gillae, '& ní imgabaim óenfer.'

'Ní tergae i tír,' ol Condere, 'corot sloindi.'

'Regad a leith dia tuidched,' ol in gillae.

Condere went thereafter and met with the boy there on the shore. 'That is sufficient to come, oh little lad,' said Condere, 'without telling us why you are coming and who your nation is.'

'I do not declare myself to one man,' said the youth, 'and I don't give way to one man.'

'You won't go to the land,' said Condere, 'without declaring yourself.'

'I will go the direction I intend,' said the youth.

Imsoí ass in mac. Is and asbert Condere:

Tinta frim, a mo maic. At morgnímach. At fola ferdamnai. Ardán errad Ulad cucut. Ardotchobra Conchobar. Cairptini cleitini a clár clé, conid san erreda Ulad úargabas. Ardotchobra Conchobar dondigis. Clúas duit, dian tóe frim. Tinta co Conchobar, co mac níthach Nessa; co Sencha mac coscrach Oilella; co Cethirn mac fáebarderg Fintain, co tenid leónas ergala; co h-Aimirgin n-éices; co

Cumscraid mórmuirnech. Mo chen, ardot-Conall-Cernach-cobra tar turtheda, ceóla, gáiri láthlond catha. Bad búadre brón la Blaí Briugaid béim sechai, cíaso láech. Dáig ní immairic ilar ruice. La so atberer. Atrachtsa fodén, Condere, co tulad co mmac argair curada. Acht bágus domsa" ol intí Condere, "tuidecht ar chend in gillai cen ulcha cen caither, acht manip erlaithe di Ultaib."

The boy turned away. Then Condere spoke: "Turn to me, oh my lad. Stay this great activity. Stay this manly feud. Pride of the Ulsetrmen equips you. Conchobar will protect you. A little chariot, light javelins, your leftside covered, with this may the Ulstermen outfit you. Conchobar will protect your meeting. Listen to you, true silence against me. Turn to Conchobar, warlike son of Nessa; of Sencha boastful son of Oilella; of Cethirn very-keen son of Fintain, of fiery wounding battle; of Aimirgin the wise; of Cumscraid of the great armies. My leader, who is guarded by Conall Cernach, a warrior's musical cry in battles. It would be a distress and confusion to break legal guesting with violence, among warriors. Because of a meeting of abundance of reproach. With this speech, he himself rises, Condere, with consent to the boy a warrior's prohibition. Therefore, it is contentious for me" said he, Condere, "meeting the arrival of a lad without a beard, without body-hair, but that is why there are not two Ulstermen."

"Is maith dondigis," ol in gillae. "Rotbíaso didiu t'acallam. Gléssiu gotha. Léicsiu úaim erchora cen imroll a cairpthinib. Comlaus cáinsreth saigthin ar cleitinib cíanaib cen ích n-errad n-aile. Bágsu ar mórgnímaib gaiscid nád ragbad nech forbais form. Fásaigseo let co hUltu in feraimsea for galaib óenfir nó for línaib fer for ndul. Soí ass doridisi", ol in gillae, "air cía no beth nert céit let, nída túalaing mo ergairi.

"Maith," ol Condere, "táet nech aile íarom dot acallaim."

Luid íarom Condere co h-Ultu & adfét in sin.

"You have met me well," said the lad. "You shall have your answer. Bright spears. A league's charge before me without a mistake to his chariot. An agreed order of soldiers shooting with little spears far away without another leader equipping them. Contentious battle without great execution of weapons and without resistence to me. I will lay waste to Ulster whether I am to fight in single combat or against many men. I am away out of it again", said the youth, "For even with powerful force assembled with you, I am not able to be prohibited."

"Fine," said Condere, "Someone else may go speak with you."

Condere went then to the Ulstermen and told them.

"Níba fír," ol Conall Cernach, "enech Ulad do breith céin am beósa." Luidseom didiu do saigid in maic.

"Is álaind do chluiche, a macáin," ol Conall.

"Níba frit bas étchiu," ol in gillae.

Ro lá in gillae cloich ina thabaill. Dosléici isind áer .i. táthbéimm, co riacht a bressim & a torann ac techt súas co Conall. Foceird Conall tar a chend. Riasiu atracht, dobert in gillae scíathraig a scéith fora láma.

"Nech aile friss!" ol Conall.

"Not true," said Conall Cernach, "Ulster's honor will not be taken while I am alive."

Then he went to the boy.

"Your playing is pretty, oh little boy," said Conall.

"Not against you will it be ugly," said the lad.

The lad took a stone and put it in his sling. He cast in the air, that is with his sling-stick, so that it's noise and it's thunder going up reached to Conall. He put Conall back on his head. Before he rose, the lad placed the shieldstrap of his shield on his arms.

"Another person against him!" said Conall.

Dorat tra gen forsin slúag fon indus sin. Boí Cú Chulainn immurgu oca chluichiu oc dul dochum in gillai, & lám Emire ingine Forgaill tara brágaid.

"Ná téig sís!" ol sí. "Mac duit fil tís. Ná fer fingail immot óenmac, co sechnam, a maic saigthig soailti. Ní soáig ná soairle coméirge frit mac mórgnímach mór ... n-esiut. Artai o ríag cnis fochlóc ót biliu, ba cotat fri Scáithchi scél. Mad Conlae céssad clár clé, comad fortamail taidbecht. Tinta frim! Cluinte mo chlois! Fó mo chosc! Bad Cú Chulainn cloadar! Atgénsa cid ainm asind ón, maso Conlae óenmac Aífe in mac fil tís," ol in ben.

He went this way mocking the host that was there. Cú Chulainn was there at the time going towards the lad, and Emir, daughter of Forgaill's arm over his neck.

"Do not go down!" she said. "A son to you is he. Do not commit parricide on your only son, avoid it, your aggressive son's life. It is not a fair fight and it is not wise to rise against your son. Turn away from hard punishing judgments, from harsh gossiping against you. If Conla suffers a bad defense, your protecting superior skill annuls it. Turn to me! Hear my voice! Good are my words! Let Cú Chulainn hear! I know what name he will declare, if he is Conla only son of Aoífe the son of yours," said his wife.

Is and sin asbert Cú Chulainn: "Coisc, a ben! Ní cosc mná admoiniur mórgnímaib asa coscur glé. Ní gníther do banchobrae. Bam gnímbúadach. Buidig ruisc ruirech. Dé fola form chnis crú cuirp Conlai. Caín súgfet gaí in cleitine cain. Cid é no beth and, a ben," ol sé, "na ngénainnse ar inchaib Ulad."

Is and sin luid sís fésin.

Then Cú Chulainn said: "Prevent, oh woman! No woman's prevention invokes great deeds in their shining correction. No deeds are in a woman's conversation. I shall have glorious deeds. Satisfying a king's eye. If the blood on me will be from the chest wound of Conla's body. Beautiful a loud-rushing spear, the little spear beautiful. If it is he who is there, oh woman," he said, "I will kill him for the honor of Ulster."

And he went down there.

"Is álaind, a macáin, in cluiche dogní," ol sé.

"Is étach for cluichesi cétamus," ol in mac bec, "nach táet dias úaib corom sloindisea dóib."

"In corob éicen mac blaicci im farradsa ón?" ol Cú Chulainn. "Atbélaesiu immurgu mani sloindi."

"Bid fír," ol in gillae.

Atnaig in mac cuici. Immustúaircet. Nos mbeir in gillae maíl fair cosin chlaidiub .i. béim co fomus.

"Is co cend in cuitbuid" ol Cu Chulainnn. "Tiagam do imthrascrud didiu!"

"It is pretty, oh little boy, the play you make," he said.

"There is jealousy on you for my play indeed," said the small boy, "that a pair of you did not come down so that I could declare myself to you."

"Would it have been a necessity to have a little boy along with this?" said Cú Chulainn. "Indeed, you shall die unless you declare yourself."

"Let it be true," said the lad.

The boy came towards him. They engaged each other. The lad struck a renowned cropping feat with his sword that is cutting away his hair.

"The mockery is on my head" said Cu Chulainnn. "Let us go wrestle together!"

'Ní rous do chris,' ol in mac. Ro gab in mac for dí chloich, co tarat Coin Culainn eter in dí choirthi fo thrí, & níro glúais in mac nechtar a dá chos dona coirthib, co ndechadar a thraigthi isna

clochaib conici a dá n-adbrond. Atá slicht a dá chos and béos. Is de atá Tráig Éise la h-Ultu. Lotar didiu isin muir do imbádud, cora mbáid in mac fo dó.

"I do not reach your chest," said the boy. The boy got on two stones, pushing Cu Culainn between the two stones three times, and without the boy moving his feet so that his two feet were in the stones up to his ankles. The track of his two feet is there and remains. This is the Tráig Éise of Ulster. They went then to the ocean to submerge each other, with the boy twice submerging him.

Luid risin mac íarom asin uisciu, coro bréc cosin gaí bulga, ar níro múin Scáthach do duine ríam in gaisced sin acht do Chon Chulainn a óenur. Dacorustar don mac tríasind uisce, co mboí a inathar foa chossaib.

Then he went after the boy in the water, until with deception the gae bulga was used, because no person had been taught that weapon by Scáthach but Cu Chulainnn alone. He shot it at the boy through the water, so that his entrails were at his feet.

"Is ed ón tra," ol sé, "náro múin Scáthach dom-sa! Mairg nom chréchtnaigis!" ol in mac.

"Is fír," ol Cú Chulainn. Gaibid in mac íarom eter a dí láim, & nos ucca co tall ass & na mbeir co tarlaic de ar bélaib Ulad.

"Aso mo macsa dúib, a Ultu," ol sé.

"Fé amai," ol Ulaid.

'It is that indeed,' he said, 'this Scáthach did not teach me! Woe that you have wounded me!' said the boy.

'It is true,' said Cú Chulainn. He took the boy then in his two arms, and carried him over there and carried him before the men of Ulster.

'Here is my son to you, oh Ulstermen,' he said.

'Woe and alas,' said the Ulstermen.

"Ocus is fír," ol in mac. "Dia mbeinnsea etraib co cend cóic mblíadan, no silsinnse firu in betha remib for cach leith & congébthe ríge co Róim. Inid ed so file and, inchoisc domsa na firu amrai fil isin bailiu, corom chelebra dóib."

Dobeir íarom a dí láim im brágaid cach fir ar úair & celebraid dia athair & atbail fo chétóir. Ro lád tra a gáir gubai & a fert & a liae ocus co cend trí tráth nícon reilcthea loíg dia mbuaib la h-Ultu in diaid.

"And it is true," said the boy. "If I had been among you for five years, I would vanquish the men of the world before you on every side and you would have kingship to Rome. Since it is this here, show to me the wonderful men that are here, that I may say farewell to them."

He placed thereafter his two hands around the necks of every man in turn and said farewell to his father and died then immediately. Then the warriors made his mourning cry and his burial mound and his stone and from the start to end of three days a calf was not near their cows in Ulster.

Aided Fergusa Maic Róich
The Death of Fergus son of Róich

The Irish text is taken from National Library of Scotland, Edinburgh, Adv. MS 72.1.40

Cid diata aided Fergusa maic Róich? Ní hansa.

Whence the death of Fergus son of Róch? Not difficult.

1 Búi Fergus for luinges i Connachtaib iarna sárugud im maccuib Usnech, úair is é in tres comairci tucad friu & Dubthach Dóeltenga & Cormac Conlonges mac Conchobair. Bátar dono uili tíar forsan loingis co cend cethri mbliadna déc & ní an dono gul ná crith leo a nUltaib, acht gul & crith gach n-oidhchi. Is é romarb Fiachraig mac Conchobair & is é romarb Geirgi mac nIlleda & as é romarb Eogan mac Durthact. Is lais tucad in táin .i. la Fergus. Mór tra do gnímaib dorine sium a tegluch Ailello & Medba & ba minca nobíd som & a muinter ar fot in tíre cena ná isin tegluch. Trícha cét rob é lín na loingsi & is é roba fer cumtha dó-som a tegluch Ailello .i. Lugaid Dailléigis .i. bráthair do Oilill in Lugaid sin.

Fergus was in exile in Connaught after his violations against the sons of Usnech; because he was [one of] the three guarantors given to them, with Dubthach Dóeltenga and Cormac Conlonges the son of Conchobar. These were all in exile in the west to the end of four years and ten, and thereupon weeping or trembling in Ulster never ceased with them, but they were weeping and trembling each night. It was he who killed Fiachra son of Conchobar, and he who killed Gerg son of Illand, and he who killed Eogan son of Durthacht. With him was brought the cattle raid, that is with Fergus. Great then the mighty deeds he did in the household of Ailill and Medb and frequently he and his people were longer in the land than in Ailill's household. Three thousand was the count of the exiles; and there was a man who was his friend in Ailill's household that is Lugaid Dalléces that is a brother to Ailill was Lugaid.

2 Bátar ann iar ngnímaib acon loch ar Mag Ái. Dúnad mór leo .i. cluichi & céti ann. Laa n-aon ann dono luid in slóg uili isi n loch dia fothrucad. 'Erg sís, a Fergus,' ar Ailill '& báid na firu!' 'Nít maith a n-usci,' ar Fergus. Luid-som sís ar ái sin. Nír fulaing a cridi do Meidb co ndechaid isin loch. Mur docúaid Fergus isin loch dorala ana mbui do grenaig & do clochaib a n-íchtar an locha co raibi for úachtar uli. Luid Medb didiu co raibi for a bruindi-sium & a gabla ime & co taircell-som in loch annsin & rogab ét Ailill. Doluid didiu súas Medb.

2. They were after deeds by the lake on Mag Ai. There was a great encampment by there that is games and racing there. One day there then the entire host went in the lake to bathe.

'Go down, O Fergus,' said Ailill, 'and submerge the men.'

'Not good in water,' said Fergus. Nevertheless, he went down there. Medb's heart could not bear that, so she went in the lake. As Fergus went into the lake, it happened that the gravel and stones at the bottom of the lake came all to the top. Medb went until she was on his breast chest and with her thighs around him and then he swam around the border of the lake and jealousy seized Ailill. Then Medb went up.

3 'Is álaind a ndogní an dam, a Lugaid, & an eilit isin loch,' ar Ailill. 'Cid nach gontar?' or Lugaid & ní tuc urcor n-imraill ríam. 'Teilg-su dún orchur forru!' ar Ailill. 'Impó m'agaid cuctha,' or Lugaid, '& tabraid gái dam.' Robúi Fergus aca nige asin loch & a bruinni fria & tucad a carpat docum Oilello co mbúi ina farrad & do teilc Lugaid urcor don gái co mbói triana druim síar sechtair.

'Doriacht an t-urchur!' ar Lugaid. 'Is fír on,' ar cách, 'atát bruindi Fergusa.'

3. 'It is splendid the actions of the stag, O Lugaid, and the doe in the lake,' said Ailill.

'Why not kill them?' said Lugaid, and he had never cast a shot that missed.

'Cast a shot at them!' said Ailill.

'Turn my face towards them,' said Lugaid, 'and bring a spear to me!'

Fergus was washing himself in the lake, and his chest against them and his chariot is brought to Ailill, so that it was near him; and Lugaid cast the lance, so that it escaped out through his back.

'The shot arrived!' said Lugaid.

'That is true,' said all 'that is the chest of Fergus.'

4 *'Trúag sin,' ar Lugaid, 'mo chomalta & m' fer cumtha do marbad dam-sa cin cinaid.' 'Mo carpat dam-sa!' ar Ailill. Téit in slóg uili for teiched, cach fer a leth fri tír etir luinges & Connachta. Gataid Fergus an gái as & teilcid a ndiaid Ailello co ndechaid tresin milcoin búi etir dá fertas in carpait. Luid Fergus íarum asin loch & nusdírgenn forsan tulaig a taeib in locha & luid a anum as focétóir & atá a lige ann fós.*

Conid hí Aided Fergusa connuici sin

4. 'How miserable,' said Lugaid, 'if I should have killed my foster-brother and my friend without intention [literally legal guilt].'

'My chariot to me!' said Ailill. The whole host went in flight, every man towards the land, both exiles and the men of Connaught. Fergus pulled out the spear and cast it after Ailill, so that it passed through the hunting dog that was between the two rear-shafts of the chariot. Whereafter Fergus came out of the lake, and straightens himself out on the hillock by the side of the lake and his soul rises out of him. And his grave is there to this day.

So this is the death of Fergus.

Athirne Áilgessach & Mider Brí Léith
Athirne Ailgessach and Midir of Bri Leith

A short tale of a stingy man with magical cranes which references the Tuatha De Danann figure Midhir who was known in later folklore as a fairy king. The Irish text is from the *Book of Leinster*.

Athirne Ailgessach mac Ferchertne. is e is doichlechu ro boi i nHerind. Dochoid co Mider Brí Léith co tuc corra diultada & doichle úad fora thech .i. ar dibe & ar dochill. Arna taidled fer do feraib Herend a thechsom do aigidecht l^ foigde. Na tair. na tair ar in chetchorr. Eirgg ass ol a setig. Sech thech sech thech ar in tres chorr. Cachfer do feraib Herend ataciched ni gebed fria chomlund a llaasin. Nocho doid a. saith riam bale i nfacced duine. Luidseom dano & mucc urgnaide leis & paitt meda co n-essad a saith a oinur. & ro chertaigestar ara belaib in muicc & in paitt meda. Co n-acca in fer chuice. Dogenta th'oínur ar se la tadall na mmuicce & na paitte uad. Cia th'ainmseo ar Athirni. Nocon erdairc ón ar se .i. Sethor. Ethor. Othor. Sele. Dele. Dreng Gerce. Mec Gerce. Ger Gér. Dír Dír iss ed mo ainmse. Ni thanic in mucc. & forfemmid inn air do chuibdigud. Dóig combad ó Dia thísta do breith na mmucce. ar nírbo anfélisium ond uairsin.

Athirne Ailgessach son of Ferchertne, he was most inhospitable in all of Ireland. He went to Midir of Brí Léith and took cranes[39] of pettiness and inhospitality from him for his house, that is stinginess and grudgingness. No man of Ireland visits his house looking for hospitality. "Do not come. Do not come" said the first crane.

"Go out!" said his companion.

"Beyond the house, beyond the house" said the third crane.

Every man of Ireland who saw them would not succeed in battle that day.

He did not eat where there were people. He went once and a prepared pig with him and a skin of mead to eat his fill alone. And he settled his mouth on the pig and the skin of mead. He saw a man coming towards him. He wanted to be alone when he was touching the pig and the skin.

"What name is on you?" said Athirni.

"Nothing famous is on me" he said "that is Sethor[40] Ethor[41] Othor[42] Sele[43] Dele[44] Dreng[45] Gerce[46] Mec Gerce[47] Ger Gér[48] Dír Dír[49] is my name."He [Athirni] didn't take [back] the pig. And he was unable to compose a satire. It is likely someone of God had come to carry away the pig. He was not ungenerous from that hour.

Athirne ocus Amairgen mac Ecet Salach
Athirneand and Amairgen Son of Ecet Salach

This story is listed in the *Ulster Cycle,* although it does not directly tie into any of the other stories there. I wanted to translate include it because I find it an intriguing piece and really enjoy the amount of description it includes. The Irish text was sourced from the *Lebar na Núachongbála*

Baí goba amra i nUltaib .i. Eccet Salach goba a ainm. Ainm n-aill do Echen. suí cech admait. conna rabi riam liarum goba bad ferr. Rucad iarum mac dó. Amairgen a ainm. Ro buí iarum in macsin i mmacrai cethéora mbliadna déc. cen labrad.

There was a famous smith in Ulster that is Ecet Salach[50] was the smith's name. His other name was Echen. Every skill was his so that before or after there was no better smith. He had a son, Amairgen was his name. The boy went fourteen years of his childhood without speaking.

Ro ás a. brú iarum combo méit adbul teig móir. & ba feithech glasremor in brúsin. & a smucli asa sróin inna beolu. Ba dub a chroccend. Batir gela a fiacla. Ba glasbán a aged. Amal da urbuinne builg goband a lurgne & a sliastai. Batir laebladracha a thraigid. Batir adbolmóra a adbronna. Batir ardda imchiana a da ngruad. Batir domna dubderga a dí súil. Ba lebormailgech anúas. Ba garb drestaide a folt. ba mellach cnámach carrgarb a druim. Nibó cáemduine samlaid. Dia follaigthe cu ciana inna suidiu cen foglanad doacmaised a múrtraide dó cotice a di leiss.

His belly grew almost as vast as a huge house and it was sinewy, thick-grey and flaking. The mucus from his nose went to his mouth. His pelt was black. His teeth were white. His face was pallid. Like the two bellow-bags of a smith were his shins and his thighs. His feet had crooked toes. His ankles were huge. Both high and very long were his two cheeks. Deep, dark red were his two eyes and drooping down. Coarse and thorny was his hair. Humped, bony and scabby was his back. Thus, he wasn't an attractive person. Because of long neglect while he was sitting without clearing away his excrement [it] would reach to his thighs.

Batír é a sercla gruth bruithe. mór luatha. mera derga. caera glassa. diasa loscthi. gais chrema. cnoi caecha a mbith for clár oca oca airfitiud.

His delicacies were cooked curds, salt, red berries, green berries, burned ears of corn, sprigs of wild garlic, empty nuts for his meal which he entertained himself with at his table.

Dofoíd iarum Athirne a gilla .i. Greth a ainm co Ecet Salach do chor béla i tenid. Co n-acca Greth in n-arracht ndóer ndochraid ísin ara chind for lar in tige. Danéci co anmín. atrágestar Greth. Buí ingen Ecit i cathair cumtachtai & tlacht derscaigthe impe issin tig. & sí a hoínur oc comét in tige. & in mac na fail. Co cualatae ní in mac fri gilla nAthirni.

Then Athirne[51] sent his servant, that is Greth was his name, to Ecet Salach to forge a battle-axe in the fire. Then Greth[52] saw the ignoble ugly spectre there before him on the floor of the house. He looked with harsh dread at Greth. Ecet's daughter was in the well-made building and a distinguished garment about her in the house. And she alone was guarding the house and the boy in his place. The boy was heard saying something to Athirne's servant.

"In n-ith Greth gruth" ol se fo thrí. Niro recart Greth. & atrágestar co mmór. Asbert im frisseom arisi. "Grínmuine gránmuine gais chrema. cuae uinn. ubla greti. gruth. in n-ith Greth gruth."

"Does Greth eat curds " he said three times. Greth didn't answer and greatly feared. He spoke to him again. "Blackberries, sloes, sprigs of wild garlic, pine nuts, apples, curds. Does Greth eat curds."

Atnaig Greth dó assin tig. conid corastar dar droichtiu ind liss. isin cechair. Luidi iar sin co rranic Athirne. "Atchonnarcais ócu" ol Athirne olc féth fil fort.

"Deithbir dam" ol Greth . "Mac cetheora mbliadan naro labrastar riam dom acallaim indiu. & fotfuicfeso in macsin cen grád mani dibdaither."

"Cid asrubairt frit" ol Athirne.

"Ni handsa" ol Greth. "In n-ith Greth. &c. Imchomairc

Greth ran from the house, with a cry across the bridge of the fort into the mud. Then he returned back to Athirne.

"He sees warriors," said Athirne "an evil appearance is on you."

"It's expected for me," said Greth. "A boy who hasn't spoken before for fourteen years spoke to me today. And unless he's removed the lad will extinguish your many ranks."

"What did he say to you" said Athirne.

"Not hard." said Greth. [does Greth eat curds etc.,]

Athirne cindas both isind liss. Adfét dó in gilla uile amal luide Greth assind liss.

Tanic Ecet fo chetoir. Asbert a ingen fris. "Ro labrastar Amargen indiu" ol si "fri gilla nAthirni dodechaid sund do denam bela lais."

"Cid asbert friss."

In n-ith Greth gruth. &c.

Athirne asked how many were in the hut with him. Greth told that the other servant went out with him.

Ecet went back to the building. His daughter spoke to him. "Amairgen spoke today," she said. "to the servant of Athirne sent here to ask you to make an axe."

"What did he say to him."

[Does Greth eat curds, etc.,]

"Bid ed bias de" ol Ecet. "Ticfa Athirne do marbad in meic arna ragba fair. ar biaid mór sóis ocun mac ro rádi in sein."

"I know what will come of this." said Ecet. "Athirne will come to kill the boy so he will not prevail over him. Because there is great wisdom with the boy who reflects on that."

Dotet ind ingen iarum cosin mac lé assind liss dond airgi buí oc Sliab Mis tess. Dogní Ecet deilb in meicc di chriaid & suidigis fo láim chlí dó etir & a builg. & dobert dagthimthach imbi. & suidigis inna liugu amal bid ina chotlud no beth.

The girl went and took the boy with her out of the fort with their herd of cows to Sliab Mis in the south. Ecet made the form of the boy from clay and set it by his left arm between him and his bellows. He placed good clothing about it. And set it sleeping as if it were a living thing asleep.

Tic Athirne iar sin & a gilla Greth. Co n-accatar in mac inna thálgud. Dognith a mbieil leo. & batar ro maith & adacht for samthaig. Dambert Athirne imma chend na delba ucut amal bed in mac beth and. & atnaig do for teiched & eigther impu.

Athirne went there then with his servant Greth. They saw the boy looking soothed. Their axe was ready for them and it was good and they took the axe. Athirne brought it down on the head of the figure there, as if doing violence to the boy's life there. And they fled the house with a cry about them.

Lotar in tsluaig ina ndiaid. Tecmalla Aithirne a folad & a inmass issin less. & gabtha fair a les. Tecait Ulaid gleithir eturru. Doberar .uii. cumala & log a einig dó & dognither cora eturru. & gaibid Athirne in mac for altram .i. Amorgen & legais suithe filidechta laiss. Conid iarum ro laig senordacht for Athirne & ro gab Amorgen ardollomnacht Ulad.

The host went after them. Aithirne assembled his wealth and his treasure there with him and secured his fort. The Ulstermen went [and] settled around him. [Ecet] was given seven cumals[53] and acquired his honour price and an agreement was made between them. And Athirne took the boy in fosterage, that is Amairgen, and he studied poetry with him. Thereafter Athirne's precious seniority was lost and Amairgen was the highest poet of Ulster.

Chapter 3

The Dindshenchas

The Dindshenchas are collections of place name stories that include a variety of mythic tales connected to specific locations. I have focused here on a handful that mention or are centred on particular members of the Tuatha De Danann or figures with similar names, such as Macha the fairy woman and Macha Mongruadh. A great deal can be learned both about the gods and aos sidhe as well as about these particular places by studying these place name stories.

Berba

A short tale of the Morrigan's son Meiche, his death, and why the river Berba is still. The Irish text is taken from Stokes, W., (1894). *The Prose Tales of the Rennes Dindshenchas.*

Berba, canas ro ainmniged?

Ni ansa. Meiche mac na Morrigna is and robatar na tri crideda, corot-marb Mac cecht im-Maig Mechi. Mag Fertaigi dano a ainm in maige co sin. Amlaidh badar na cride sin, co ndelbaib tri nathrach treithib. Meni torsed dano bas do Mechi arforbertais na nathracha ind & focnafed ana faigbet béo i nHérinn. Roloisc iarum Mac cecht inna cride sin im-Maig Luathat, coro la al-luaith lasin sruth, conid romarb eas in tsrotha, ocuscoro marb cach n-anmanda roboi ann, ocus coro mberb. Nó combad i n-Aird Luaithrid noloisc. Unde Berba dicitur ocus Mag Meche ocus Aird Luaithrid. Nó comad Berba .i. ber nó bir ocus ba .i. balb. Unde Berba dicitur .i. usce balb.

Berba, why this name?

Not difficult. Meiche was a son of the Morrigan and he had three hearts, until he was killed by Mac Cecht at Maige Mechi. Maige Fertaigi was the name of the plain before that. This way were those hearts, with three forms of three serpents. Moreover, if not for the death of Meiche, the serpents would have grown to the end and consumed therefore all life in Ireland. Then Mac Cecht burned the hearts there at Maig Luathat, throwing the ashes in the course of the river, so that the rapids in the stream died, and brought death to every animal there and boiling. Or else he may have destroyed them in Ard Luaithard (or he burned them). So Berba is said and Mag Meche and Ard Luauthrid.

Or it's called Berba, that is ber or bir – water – and ba that is balb – silent – whence Berba is called silent water.

Odras

A more involved place name story about the river Odras, which describes what happens when a human woman tries to steal back her cows which have been stolen from her by the Morrigan. The Irish text is from E. Gwyn, 1906

Odras, úais ind ingen,
fris' indlem laíd lúaidme,
Odornatan airme
meic Laidne meic Lúaidre.

Odras, noble the woman,
about whom we make this poem,
daughter of famed Odornatan
son of Laidne son of Lúaidre.

Ban-briugaid ba brígach
in gnímach glan gúasach,
céile cáem co cruthacht
do Buchatt balcc búasach.

A wealthy woman and powerful
the active, pure, danger-loving,
beloved and fair wife
of stout cattle-lord Buchatt.

Bóaire cáid Cormaic
co roblait in Buchatt,
dúiscid búar co m-blaitne
cach maitne for muchacht.

Stock-master to noble Cormac
was the strong Buchatt,
he awakens the mighty herds
each morning early.

Fechtus luid dia ésse
a ben glésse gasta,
Odras rúad co romét,
do chomét búar m-blasta.

One day went journeying out
his bright, alert wife,
Odras fierce and proud,
to guard the fair cattle.

Moch dia m-boí 'na codlud
Odras groc-dub gnóach,
dosrocht ben in Dagda,
ba samla día sóach.

Early in the day slept
Odras, dark-wrinkled, beautiful,
[then] the wife of the Dagda came,
a phantom the shape-shifting Goddess.

Tuc léi tarb in tnúthach,
in rígan garb gnáthach,
baí i Líathmuine láthach,
in fíachaire fáthach.

She took with her a furious bull,
the well-known harsh queen,
from Líathmuine of mighty deeds,
the wise raven-prophesier.

Dairis boin in búaball,
tarb túamann 'nar taídenn,
ó Themraig tric táraill
co Slemnaib Fraích Oírenn.

The bull covered a cow,
a bull of grave-mounds and hosts,
traveled swiftly from Tara
to Oírenn's smooth moorland.

Slemon ainm in tairb-sin,
dremon in dóel donn-sin:
a ainm, mer cen mebsain,
'sed rolen in fonn-sin.

Slemon was the name on the bull,
furious the swarthy black one:
his name, spirited without defeat,
remained with that territory.
Luid co Crúachain cróda

iarsind úath-blaid ágda
in Mórrígan mórda,
ba slóg-dírmach sámda.

To bloody Crúachan she went
thereafter the great war-like phantom,[54] the mighty Mórrígan,
whose ease was a host of troops.

Luid Odras 'na h-iarn-gait,
iarmairt nárbu ada,
's a gilla dúr dorthain,
torchair i Cúil Chada.

Odras came to thieve with iron,
not a justified consequence,
with her solid, unlucky servant,
who accidently fell at Cúil Chada.

Cada ainm a gilla
rofinna mór fíche:
ruc Odras, úair áithe,
for lurg a búair bíthe.

Cada was her servant's name
he knew great fights:
Odras brought him, a swift hour,
in pursuit of her taken cows.

Iarsin, d' éis a gilla,
luid in ben gléis glanda
co Síd Crúachan cumma,
co fríth úath-blad alla.

Thus, after her servant's death,
came the bright, pure woman
to Sídhe Crúachan's form,
in wilderness a great phantom hall.

Roléic cotlud chuicce
in groc-dub cen glicce
i nDaire úar Fhálgud
dia fúair sárgud sicce.

She allows sleep to take her
the dark-wrinkled one without wisdom
at unfriendly Daire Fhálgud
there she is overtaken by cold dishonouring

Dosruacht ina tathum,
trúag tachur for tulaig,
in Mórrígan úathmar
a h-úaim Chrúachan cubaid.
Came upon her sleeping,
returning on the hill,
the Mórrígan, great phantom,
her cave is fittingly Crúachan.

Rochan fuirre ind agda
tria luinde cen logda
cach bricht dían, ba dalbda,
fri Slíab mBadbgna m-brogda.

Chants over her the possessor of the cows
with vehemence unabating
each swift spell, it was sorcery,
towards mighty Slíab Badbgna.

Legais in ben brígach
fri Segais, sreb súanach,
mar cach linn cen líg-blad:
nísbaí brígrad búadach.

Dissolves the vigorous woman
against Segais, a sleepy stream,
like every pool without famed-stone:
she had no victorious powers.

Don tshruthán fháen fhoglas
is ainm sáer co soblas,
luid ón mnaí thrúaig thadaill
cosin abainn Odras. O.

There a prone greenish stream
is named, noble and sweet-tasting,
this wretched woman becomes
the little river Odras there.

Noínden Ulaid
Debility of the Ulstermen

Explaining why it is that the men of Ulster are cured with weakness when in their greatest hour of need, a key factor setting up Cu Chulainn's solitary defence of Ulster during the Táin Bó Cuiliagne. The Irish text is from the *Prose Dindshenchas*

Ailiter: Machae dano ben Chruind meic Agnoman doriacht and do comrith fri heacha Concobair, ar atbert an fer ba luaithiu a bean. Amlaid dano bói in ben, is hi inbadhach, cor chuinnigh cairde coro thoed a brú, ocus ni tucad di, ocus dognith in comrith iarum, ocus ba luaithem si, ocus o ro siacht (cenn) in céiti beridh mac ocus ingen - Fir ocus Fial a n-anmand - ocus atbert co mbedis Ulaid fo ceis óited in cach uair dus-ficfad eicin. Conid de bái in cess for Ulltaib fri re nomaide o flaith Concobair co flaith Mail meic Rochraidhe, ocus atberet ba hí sin Grian Banchure ingen Midir Brí Léith, ocus atbeb iar suidhiu, ocus focresa a fert i nArd Machae ocus focer a guba ocus roclannuadh a líae. Unde Ard Macha

Furthermore: Macha, moreover, wife of Chruind son of Agnoman who arrived there to race against the horses of Conchobar, because her husband had said his wife is quicker. Thus moreover was the woman, she is due for delivery, she seeks a surety compact[55] to bring forth her womb, and none is given, and she is brought to race therefore, and she is the quicker, and when she reaches the (head of) the assembly she bears a son and a daughter - Fir [True] and Fial [Honorable] were their names - and she said that the Ulstermen would be under a complaint of youth in each when their enemies compelled them. Therefore, was this debility on the Ulstermen for nine days and nine nights from the rule of Conchobar to the rule of Mail son of Rochraidhe, and it is said she was Grian Banchure [Sun of

Womanhood] daughter of Midir of [the sídhe of] Brí Léith, and she died then after that and they put her burial mound in Ard Macha and performed her mourning lament and placed her stone. Whence Ard Macha [Macha's Height].

Emain Macha
The Story of the Name of Emain Macha

How Emhain Macha – modern day Navan Fort – got its name through the actions of the pseudo-historical queen Macha Mongruadh and her quest to rule after her father's death. The Irish text is taken from Irish from Meyer, K., (1907) Archiv für Celtische Lexikographie

---

Cid diatá Eomuin Machae? Ni hanse. Bui righi n-Erenn hi comflaithius etir Ruad mac m-Bodhuirn & Cimbaeth mac Finntain & Dithorbae mac Dimain. Secht m-bliedna do cech oe hi flaith h-Erenn. Imcloeth beus hi cinn hsecht m-bliada na. Ocus is amlaid do-faspenta a righe do flaith nod-gebed beus: 'Ind flaith si do-asselbtur duit a taspenad uait a n-ógi .i. dom-biur duit cen gái cen ethech cen imarbae cen anfir flatha. Glinne aurut friss .i. secht n-octhigerna & secht righ (no druith) & secht file .i. na h-oigthigirn dot fognam, na druith dot ressadh & dott imdergadh, na filid dott aorad tre m-bricht co rabuit i talmain ria nomaide'. Is amlaid sin tra do-aissilbith ind flaith co m-betiss immurgu na torthae iarna coir lasna flaithi. Is aire dognidiss in sin.

Why the name of Emhain Macha? Not difficult. There were kings in Ireland who shared the sovereignty between them: Ruad mac m-Bodhuirn and Cimbaeth mac Finntain and Dithorbae mac Dimain. Seven years to each one ruling Ireland. Well-known to this day that division of seven years. And it is thus a king announces he possesses his sovereignty: "The point of his sovereignty assigned a few requirements of his perfection, that is judging to you without lying, without perjury, without deceit, without unjust sovereignty. A security with them against him that is seven young lords and seven kings (or druids) and seven poets, that is the the young lords to be in servitude, the druids to satirize him and to embarrass him, the poets to insult his battle prowess so that he is in earth before a period of nine days and nights". It is thus that it is throughout the parts of the world concerning sovereignty, later they are struck with correct sovereignty. A nobleman's making is in that.

Marb iar suidhiu Dithorba mac Demain, co n-gabsat a mec a forba flatha .i. Baeth & Brass & Betach & Uallach & Borbchass coic maic Dithorbai maic Demain. Do-rochair lobra dano for Ruad mac m-Boduirn, diata Ess Ruaid isin tuaiscert. Ni farcuib side cloinn inge aoninginnamma. Macha a h-ainm-sidhe. O ssniastar side in flaith {MS page 69} a comarbus a h-athar nissnarroet Cimbaeth i comflaithius. 'Do-ber-sa dam-sa illau catha', ol sissi. Do-gnither son & feguir cath eturru & memaid for Cimbaeth. Gebaid si in flaith co cend secht m-bliadan. Tanic do Chimbaeth aimserá na flatha.

Then Dithorba mac Demain died, with his sons to take the completion of his sovereignty that is Baeth and Brass and Betach and Uallach and Borbchass the five sons of Dithorbai maic Demain. A sickness fell besides upon Ruad mac m-Boduirn, named Ess Ruaid in the north. Beside him consequently his family was a daughter, his only child. Macha was her name. She rose up therefore in sovereignty in succession of her father; unwilling was Cimbaeth to be in shared sovereignty.

'Ni bera', ol in ingen, 'conidruca ar ecin'.

Fechuir cadh ann eturrua. Memaid for Cimbaeth. Geabuid si danoflaithius co cenn secht m-bliadan. Tanic co maccuib Dithorbae in sel flatha. Feruid si cadh friu. Maidid rempe-si. Do meil si dano flaithius Dithorbai. Luid Cimbaeth cuice-si co m-bu he a fer & gaibid sí righi n-Erenn.

"I will give battle", said she.

They make a return and fierce battle between them and Cimbaeth flees. She was then in sovereignty for seven years. After this time the sovereignty was to go to Cimbaeth.

"It was not appointed", said the maiden, "but granted in the compulsion of battle".

Fierce battle there between them; defeat for Cimbaeth. She captures then his sovereignty period of seven years. The sovereignty went with the sons of Dithorbae in turn. She supplies battle against them. They flee before her. She then consumes the sovereignty of Dithorbai. Cimbaeth goes towards her with his possessions [and becomes] her husband and she takes possession of the rulership of Ireland.

Lottar maic Dithorbae for fogail & ba trom in chaladfhogal. Cech mac uilc robai ind-Eire do-choid chuca. In baile hi fuacartais nofhoglatiss ann. Ro-hearbad dano h-uadi-si naonbur cech tuaithe for a n-iarair ocus do rimarta geill cecha feine di-si dar cenn na n-drochmac batar forsan b-fogail. Con-dahualgnigset a feine ar a tuidecht dia m-bailib, co na rabadar maic Dithorbai acht a n-aonur .i. a coic. Maoite a fogalsum anacumauc asennud.

The sons of Dithorbae go to raiding and hard living in a raiding-place. Each unlucky son who is in Ireland goes hence. They proclaim a settlement there. They trust no one as all people are seeking them and counting pledges against them from her and on behalf of the bad sons who are pillaging. In their pride they themselves battle when arriving in their own land where they are sons of Dithorbai, but they are alone and in secret. Their goods were wretched plunder in the end.

Luid si iarum feisin for a n-iarair indhi Macha a h-aonar ocus facbais Cimbaeth ina suidiu & indleatha taos secuil impi-si & ceirt impi & ballan mor ina laim & lauidi fo h-Erinn for a n-iarir, co ro-tuarascfat adi i m-Buirind Connacht. Al-luide ina n-diaid isin dithrub con[...] arnic iman tenid. Suidid accu ocon tene & at-luidestar comruc friu nacha teostaiss co in a h-aenur.

She goes afterwards herself searching for them; Macha, she alone, leaving Cimbaeth established she divides rye dough about herself and rags about her and great blemishes on her hands and sets out across Ireland seeking them. Beginning in the north-west for that reason in the region of Connacht. She went after that to a wilderness with [...] she finds their fire. They were in that place with a fire and move to fight any who have gone there alone.

'Can do-dechad, a banscal?' ol in oig.

'Is do cein & fhogus on', ol sisi.

Do-berat biad di & doim-gairett dul chuice.

'Nato', ol sisi. 'Caillech amnachtach truagh, ni coir mu t-saurugad.'

'Con-ricfa fri firu anocht, a chaillech', ol seat. 'Cia raghas chuice a tosaig?'

'Misi', ol in sindsir .i. ol Baeth. Luid side focetoir. Do-bert a sliasait dar a braguit.

'Fe amai!' ol se, 'marb amin ben ocaib.'

"What brings you, oh woman?" said the youths.

"I'm always without and in injured disgrace", said she. They give food to her and laugh, going towards her.

"By no means", said she. "A foolish, wretched old woman, it's not proper for you to violate me."

"Join with us against your fulfilment[56] tonight, oh old woman", said he. "Who will choose to begin with her?" "Me", said the eldest, that is said Baeth. She goes freely. She brings him as a hostage with her two thighs.

"Woe, alas" said he, "deadly thus an exalted woman."

'At fer trogh', ol Brass. Luid side don cennu. Do-ber si dano a cois tar suide. Ticc a ceile. Fo-rurmed [...] dano. Tecuit uile & at-raig forru & ataig lomain forra .i. [...] uile ocus imatacht reimpi co rainic Eamuin [...] dia marbad.

"I'll go after the embarrassed man", said Brass. She goes to the place apart. Takes she then the feet of the aforementioned. He becomes her servant. For [...] then. She goes to each and overcomes them and impels ropes on them that is [...] each and binds in ropes until they reach Eamuin [...] for the purpose of killing.

'Nato', ol sisi. 'Oc saighid a cirt robatar. Is anbfir a marbad. Do-berthar immurgu fo daoire di foghnum dam-sa.'

'Cissi daoire do-berthar forru? Is anfir a [...] daorad [...]

'Is fior', ol si. 'Claidid dano in raith immácuairt.'

Suidid forro & eo gairid ina laim & do fóruinn impi toraind na ratha & ro cechladar maic Dithorba inn raith .i. int eo argait ro boi do-rat dar a muin oc torainn na ratha. Conid de sin ata Eamuin Macha inghine Ruaidhi & rl. Finit.

"By no means", said she. "Is this advancing correctness. Their killing would be an injustice. Bring them together under unfreeness from service to me."

"How long will unfreeness be carried on them? It's an injustice his [...] servitude [...]

'It's a surety'' said she. "They will dig then the circumference trench of the fort"

She arranges them and calls her brooch to her hand and to the rocks about her outlines the fort and gives tidings to the sons of Dithorba of the fort, that is the silver brooch given, me thinks, from her neck which outlined the fort. Thus, is it Emain Macha for the daughter of Ruaidhi. The end.

Brug Na Bóinde II

Some interrelated stories of places around Newgrange and figures, including the Dagda, the Morrigan, Cermait, and Oengus mac ind Óg, associated with them. Contains some intriguing material. The Irish text is taken from Gwyn's *Metrical Dindshenchas*

A chóemu Breg, bríg nad bréc,
co rinnib reb, rígda in rót:
in eol dúib senchas cech thuir
fuil sund i m-Bruig mic ind Óc?

Oh nobles of Breg, authority[57] without deceit,
With sharp feats, royal the road:
The knowledge on you of every lords' story
Who are here in Brug meic ind Óc?[58]

Fégaid in síd ar bar súil,
is fodeirc dúib, is treb ríg,
rogníth lasin Dagda n-dúr,
ba dín, ba dún, amra bríg.

Observe the sidhe[59] before your eyes,
It is conspicuous to you, a king's holding
Built by the resolute[60] Dagda,
It is a defence, it is a fort, marvellously strong

Fégaid Imdai n-Dagdai deirg:
forsind leirg, cen galmai n-gairg;
rofer surge sóir iar seilg
fri mnái cóim cen meirg cen mairg.

Observe, Bedroom of the red Dagda,
Above the hillside, without rough harshness;
He nobly courted[61] after a hunt
A fair woman without defeat, without sorrow.

Fégaid Dá Cích rígnai ind ríg
sund iar síd fri síd-blai síar:
áit rogénair Cermait cóem
fégaid for róen, ní céim cían:

Observe [the] Two Breasts of the king's queen
They are beyond the sidhe west of the sidhe-plain:
Place [of] fair Cermait's birth
Observe on the path, not a far step:

Dia luid ben mic Námat náir
i n-dáil ar chend Dagdai déin,
ocus in cú in a díad,
ciarbo thurus cian do chéin:

When came the wife of the son of noble Nemed
Going to meet with the swift Dagda
And the hound following after her,
Though a long journey from afar:

Dia luid Midir a Brí Léith
fri tócbáil tréith, ba fó fríth:
co tuc mac ind Oc ónd áth
co scíath 'na scáth, ciarbo scíth.

When came Midhir of Bri Leith
To take away[62] a weak one,[63] it was lucky
He went with the mac ind Óc[64] from the ford
With a shield of his protection, though he was tired.

Iarsain tucad, cialla cor,
in mac dia nói m-bliadna m-bil.
coa athair, ba cadla gair,
dia thaig cosin Dagda n-dil.

Afterwards they came, a significant contract,
The son [that] day nine good years [after]
To his father, a beautiful command,
To the house of the beloved Dagda

Dogníth ergnam leis dond ríg
isin tshíd, tre brégrad m-búan,
de atá, ní ceist cen rún,
Duma Treisc ar súil na slúag.

A feast was prepared for him by the king
Within the sidhe, through unfailing excellence,
So it is, no question without a mystery,
Duma Treisc[65] before the eyes of the hosts.

Iarsin dlomais Dagda dúr
asa dún, níb adba m-bróin,
co m-bái i n-Ochun, fecht co núaill,
iar n-othur slúaig, iar u-úair óil.

Afterwards the resolute Dagda turned him out
From his fort, no abode of sorrow,
And he lived in Ochan,[66] a famed journey,
After warlike labour, after a time of drinking

Ferta Escláim, érimm sruith,
a telctís cesta fir maith,
fót co m-balc-raind, gním cen chleith,
do mac Calpraind ba rót raith.

Grave of Esclam, esteemed journey.
Where questions are cast by good men,
Territory of vigorous portions, feats without concealing,
For the son of Calpurn it was a path of grace.

In eol dúib Derc m-Buailc bil
comarba fil immon mag,
asa n-ésib loimm lúath lib
a dig don tshlúag, fíad-glonn glan.

Is the knowledge on you of [the] Well[67] of good Bualc
Successor through the plain,
Out of which he sipped quickly
His drink for the host, a pure honourable-deed

In eol dúib Lecht Cellaig crúaid
co núaill ellaig, erctha gáeth:
atbath tre beirt láechda lúaith,
dia m-bói thúaith for báeth-bla báeth.

Is the knowledge on you of [the] Grave of harsh Cellach
With cries in unison, fills the wind:
Dying through a swift heroic pair,
When he was in the north on a foolish unwise act.

In eól dúib Lecht Gabra ind ríg
Cinaeda cen galma gráin;
ruc búaid a siblachaib sréin
do réir mic Irgalaig áin.

Is the knowledge on you of [the] Grave of the Horse of the king
Cinaed without harsh terror:
He took victory from swift-moving ones of the bridle
By the will of [the] son of splendid Irgalach

A Cír a Currel na mná,
cia bale itá cechtar de,
méraid ó 'ndiu co tí bráth;
ní ba messu ar chách a n-gné.

That Comb, that Casket[68] of the woman
Wherever either of them is,
They will remain until Doomsday
They will not be judged less in form

Fégaid lib, ba bág cech báird,
ba fert fir áin, fuaim cen meirg,
fuirglid, is íath n-gáela gairg,
síd æda Lurgnig for leirg.

Observe before you, it was a boast of every bard,
It was [the] grave of a splendid man, sound without decay
Witness, it is a land of rough kin,
[the] feiry sidhe of Lurgnech on the hillside

And dogníth rúamna dia thríath
for cúan-bla clíach ocus crích;
ba h-ed slóg-dígal na túath,
Mórrígan múad áitt i m-bíth.

There was done bloodshed[69] by a lord
On the resort of ridges and territories:
There was the host-vengeance of the people
[the] glorious Morrigan was in life there[70]

In eól dúib tre gnímrad n-gnáth,
fri fáth fír-glan, fichtib tríath,
iath n-acht-glan i m-bátar scéith,
Carcar ind Léith i m-bái in Líath.

Is there knowledge on you of famous feats,
Towards pure-truth knowledge, scores of lords,
Territory of the bright-acts in which were shields,
Prison of the Greyness in which was the Grey.

In eól dúib tre chátha cend
in glend i m-bíd Mátha mall?
robíth iar n-inriud slóg seng;
dogníth mór do imniud and.

Is the knowledge on you of battle slaughter[71]
The glen in which dwelt sluggish Matha?[72]
It was after the invasion of the graceful host
Great sorrow was made there

Iarsin tictís, gním cen chleith,
ind ríg dia leith ó thír thoich,
do descin in Máthai múaid,
co cland cách fair crúaid a chloich.

Afterwards came, feat without hiding,
The kings from a pleasing land because of him,
To gaze upon the noble Matha,
Each drove in[73] on him cruelly his stone

Clandais Buide a liic laind
'sind raind forsmbíd Suide Find:
fácaib fiad churib na n-glend
a chend for Maig Murid mind.

Buide drove in his eager stone
There in the portion at Finn's Seat:
He left, in the presence of troops of the glen,
His head on the honourable plain of Murid

Iarsin lotar Ulaid uill
Leth cubaid Cuinn ar a chend,
do gleic fri nert Máthai maill,
combrúithe a baill for Leicc Bend.

Afterwards came the great Ulstermen
Conn's proper portion against him
To contest against [the] strength of Sluggish Matha,
His organs[74] were boiled[75] on Lecc[76] Benn[77]

Doringned leo duma n-dúr
do múr for cnámaib in míl:
ba hé in coscur, fecht co núaill,
rothecht fri búaid ocus bríg.

A solid mound was built by them
An embankment over the bones of the creature:
That was the triumph, a hosting with cries,
Possessed with victory and splendor

Caisel n-Oengussa cen chol,
Airther[78] *n-Oenlussa rodlen:*
mic Crundmáil forsndessid cin
dia n-essib mid corbo mer.

Stone fort of Oengus without guilt[79]
Airther of Oenlussa[80] clung to it
Guilt settled on the son of Crundmael
When he drank mead until he was crazy

Forsin Róot rígda in gleó
in mic Óoc, cid dia m-bói?
dia robriss súil Midir múaid,
in fail úaib nech asidchói?

Upon royal pathway the combat
The meic Óc, what cause was it?
When the eye of glorious Midhir was broken,
Is there any among you who can tell it?

Mag Muirthemne

A short piece from volume 4 of the *Metrical Dindshenchas* which covers a fascinating incident with the Dagda.

Magh Muirtemne, cidh diatá? Ní ansa. Tricha blíadan íar n-dilind baí muir thairis, conidh de adberar Murthemne de. .i. temhe (?) in mara, nó fo scemil mara h-é. Nó mur draidhechta baí fair co muir-selche ann co n-aicnedh suightheach lais. Consuighedh in fer cona armgaiscedh chuige, co m-bidh for lár a ustudh-builg. Co táinic in Dagdha & a lorg anfaidh 'na laim & rothom uadh for an muir-tshelche & rochan na bríathra-sa. 'Taí do chenn cúasachtach. Taí do chorp císachtach. Toí do thul toghuidhe. Báig thúaigh.' Co rothraigh an muir-tshelche desin cosin muir n-druidhechta & comadh desin adbertha Mag Murthemne de.

Mag Muirthemne, whence is it named? Not difficult. Thirty years after the flood the sea was over it, so it is called Muirthemne, that is darkness of the sea, or under cover of the sea it was. Or there was a magical sea over it with a sea-monster there with the property of suction on it. It would suck in a man with armour on him, until he was on the interior of its craw.[81] The Dagda came and his Lorg Anfaidh[82] in his hand and he aims at the sea-monster and chants the words, "Turn your cavernous head. Turn your dirty body. Turn your hollow forehead. Curving battle." Then the sea-monster retreated[83] along with the magical sea and [this is] maybe also [why] it is called Mag Muirthemne.

Tond Clidna I
Cliodna's Wave I

A story of the Tuatha De Danann woman Cliodhna and how she came to be associated with a specific area in Cork. The Irish text is from Irish from the *Metrical Dindshenchas*.

Clidna chend-fhind, búan a bét,
'con tuind-se tánic a héc;
damna d'a máthair beith marb
inní dia tarla in sen-ainm.

Cliodna Fair-Haired, eternal her exploits,
with this wave came her end;
the cause of her mother's death
this the matter of the ancient name.

Dia ndernad in t-óenach the
ac lucht tíre tairngire,
is é thuc in mnái tre cheilg,
Ciabán mac Echach imdeirg.

When there was held the gathering of the
people of the land of promise,
it is he who took the woman through deception,
Ciabán son of Echach Imdeirg.

Rígan ind óenaig thall tra,
ingen dar' chomainm Clidna,
tar in ler lethan longach
tuc leis Ciabán cass-mongach.

The Queen of the gathering in truth,
the maiden her name was Cliodna,
taken over the ship-full ocean
taken with Ciabán curly-haired.

Rofhácaib hí forsin tuind,
luid uaithi echtra n-étruimm,
d'iarraid selga, monur mass,
luid roime fon fhid fholt-chass.

he left her on the waves,
he went on a swift adventure,
he sought to hunt, fine work,
he went forth under the foliage, the curly-haired.

Tánic in tond tara éis,
do Chiabán nírbo deg-shéis;
mór gním, ba dimda linne,
bádud Clidna cend-fhinde.

the wave came after he left,
to Ciabán no well-omened sound;
great acting, that inhospitable ocean,
Drowned was Cliodna Fair-haired.

Tond dúine Téite na tríath,
issé a hainm roime in bar n-íath
nocorbáided 'mon tuind tra
ben diarbo chomainm Clidna.

The wave of the People of Téite of the lords,
was its name before in this territory
Until in truth the wave drowned
a woman there who was named Cliodna.

Lecht Téite 'sin tráig-se túaid;
rogáet immese a mór-shlúaig;
lecht Clidna 'sin tráig-se thess,
fri Síd Duirn Buide anairdess.

Téite's grave and her strand are northwards;
she was slain amidst her great army;
Cliodna's grave and her strand are southward,
southeast of the Sídhe of Duirn Buide.

Fliuchthar folt in Duirn Buide
i tondaib in trom-thuile:
cid dimda do neoch fuil ann,
is sí Clidna nosbáidenn.

Wet is the hair of Duirn Buide
in the waves of the heavy tide:
yet displeasure to anyone's blood there,
it is Cliodna that was drowned.

Ildathach is a dá macc,
robáitea in triur ac tochmarc;
is mairg roadair don luing
náchasanaig ar óen-tuind.

Ildathach and his two sons,
were drowned the three while courting;
There is sorrow to those who cleaved to the ship
who weren't saved from one wave.

Cóica long lótar tar sál,
teglach tige Manannán;
nocharb í 'n chongaib cen gá:
robáitea ar thondaib Clidna. C.

fifty ships went across the sea,
the household of the house of Manannán;
That wasn't a host without spears:
they were drowned in the waves of Cliodna.

Tlachtga (1)

The first of two versions of how the hill of Tlachtga in Athboy gained its name. although tlachtga may be seen as a goddess and likely originally was in this tale she is a human woman who studies magic with her father, creates a fantastic device, is raped, and dies on the hill bearing three sons. The Irish text is from Irish from Kilbride MS 3, Advocates' Library, Edinburgh

---

Tlachtga can as ro hoinmniged. ní annsa. Tlachtga ingen moga Roith fordosreiblengadar trí meic Símóin druad dia luid le [a] hathair do foglaim druidechta in airther in betha. fo deig is í doróine [ms. doroighne] in roth rámach do Thriun ocus in lia i Forchartha ocus in coire i Cnámchoill. térnái iaram anair ocus in dede sin lé go torracht telaigh Tlachtga. fordoslamnadh ann sin iarum go mberdais trí macu. i. Dorib diatá magh nDoirbi. ocus Cuma diatá mag Cuma. ocus Muach diatá mag Muich. i céin dana beid an anmann sin i cuimni fer nEirenn ní thora dígal nechtrann dochum nEirenn. ocus atbath dia hassaidh ocus is uirri dorinnedh in dún . unde Tlachta. Tlachtga ingen Mogha móir . rosleblengadar meic Símóin ; ó'n nuair thánic dar muir mas . is di atá Tlachtga taebghlas

Tlachtga, why this name on it? Not difficult. Tlachtga daughter of Mog Roith who was assaulted by the three sons of Simon Magus when she went with her father to study magic in the east of the world. It was she for the sake of Thriun who constructed the oared wheel and the stone that is Forchartha and the cauldron that is Cnamhchoill. She escaped afterwards from the east and with the two at Tlachtga discharged her illegitimate birth. She delivered there afterwards the three sons she was carrying that is Dorib from whom is magh nDoirbi [plain of

Dorib]. And Cuma from whom is magh Cuma [plain of Cuma]. And Muach from whom is magh Muich [plain of Muach]. As long as these names endure in the minds of the men of Ireland no onslaught of avenging foreigners will come to Ireland. And she died in childbed and over her the fort was raised, hence Tlachtga. Tlachtga daughter of great Mog. Assaulted by the sons of Simon. Over her went the great sea, that is the populace that was at Tlachtga.

Moghruith .i. Roth mac Righuill ronalt is de ba mogh Ruith. nó mogh roth .i. magus rotarum [ms. rotharam] .i. is a rothaib dognídh a thaisceladh

Mog Roth that is Roth son of Ruilt fostered him, so he is a servant of Roth. Or mogh roth that is magus rotharum that is by wheels he made his prognostications.

Mogruith mac Cinisc meic Fhirdechet .m. Forgib .m. Firglain .m. Fhírfhalaid .m. Chaeir .m. Fergusa .m. Róig .m. Rosa .m. Rudraige

Mogruith son of Cinisc son of Fhirdechet son of Forgib son of Firglain son of Fhírfhalaid son of Chaeir son of Fergusa son of Róig son of Rosa son of Rudraige

Cacht ingen Chatmainn ben eile d'Fergus máthair Mogaruith meic Fergusa ocus Roth mac Riguill rsnalt. Dér ocus Droigen máthair dá mac Mogaruith .i. Buan ocus Fercorb ocus máthair Chairbri lifechair

Cacht daughter of Chatmainn, other wife of Fergus, mother of Mog Roth son of Fergus and Roth son of Reguill who fostered him. Dér and Droigen are the mothers of Mog Roth's two sons that is Buan and Fercorb and mothers of Cairbre lifechair.

Tlachtga (2)

The second story of Tlachtga offering a slightly different view of the events, although the broad strokes remain the same. The Irish text is taken from Irish from Gwynn's Metrichal Dindshenchas

---

Tlachtga, tulach ordain úais,
forbaid mór ríg co rochrúais,
ón chéin rosgab Tlachtga thoich,
ingen Moga réil ríg-Roith.

Tlachtga, dignified, noble hillock,
[place of] completion of kings with great valour,
that long ago belonged to fair Tlachtga,
daughter of the pure servant of king Roith

Mug Roith mac Fergusa Fáil
mac Rossa rígda ronáir,
Cacht ingen Chathmind na cles
a máthair dath-grind díles.

Mug Roith son of Fergusa Fáil
son of royal, devout Rossa,
Cacht daughter of Chathmind of the feats
[was] his mother lovely-complexioned, reliable.

Roth mac Riguill roalt h-é;
de ba Mug Roith rogaide:
dá mac Moga, Búan is Chorb,
sona dar slúag a sáer-dord.

Roth son of Riguill fostered him;
so he was taken as Roth's servant:
Moga's two sons were Búan and Corb,
lucky for the host was their noble-chanting.

Ba h-í máthair na mac mass
Derdraigen dúr dron-amnass,
ocus máthair chert Cairpri,
is becht lem ó bláth-bairdni.

The mother of these sons was
Derdraigen, severe, ruthless,
and mother of fair Cairpri,
who is surely gentle as bardcraft's flower.

Ingen Moga, mílib slúag,
Tlachtga toga, nár tháeb-fhúar,
luid ria h-athair n-dímór n-dil
co Símón sáer sechtmisid.

Moga's daughter, assembly of thousands,
chosen Tlachtga, not cold her form,
went with her great and beloved father
to noble Símón sechtmisid

Trí meic la Símón, ba sám,
ba dímór a n-díabul-bág,
Nero, Carpent is Uetir,
ba balc-gent co m-beó-gletin.

Three sons had Símón, they were at ease,
vast their devilish undertaking,
Nero, Carpent and Uetir,
they were a powerful people, always in strife.

Doratsat na meicc 'malle
seirc do Thlachtga tri tháide,
cor' sílsat a broinn, cen bréic,
do chloinn chomadais chomméit.

Together the sons gave
love to Tlachtga through secrecy,
cast their seed into her womb, without exaggeration,
with fitting children of equal size.

Tlachtga di thriun, nírbo thimm,
dorigne in roth rúad rogrinn
maróen la Mug n-dímór n-dil
is la Símón sechtmisid.

Tlachtga with the three, not feeble,
she made the red wheel, greatly-strong,
together with great and beloved Mug
and with Símón sechtmisid.

Hí dorat léi in fuidell, fiss,
forfácaib in roth rochliss,
lía foirbthe i Forcarthain fainn,
ocus in coirthe i Cnámchaill.

She takes the remainder, I know,
Left behind by the wheel's track,
a perfect stone in weak Forcarthain,
and the standing stone in Cnámchaill.

Dall cach óen nodnaicfe sell,
bodar cach óen nodcluinenn,
marb risa m-benfa ní de,
don roth garb-grennach gráinne.

Totally blind each one who beholds with his eye,
deaf each one who hears it,
dead any because of the thing,
the wheel rough-bristling points.

Iar tuidecht anair don mnaí
ruc tri maccu co mór-gnaí:
atbath dia m-breith in mer menn:
scél mór cen chleith rocluinemm.

After arriving from the east
carrying three sons of great-beauty:
the bright spirited lady dies at the time of birthing:
a great story without concealing the hearing.

Anmann na mac, lúad nad chres,
Múach is Chuma is Doirb díles:
in tshlóig ó Thoraig, rostecht,
dóib (is comaid) a cloistecht.

The names of her sons, told without restriction,
Múach and Chuma and fair Doirb:
the assembly of Thoraig, possessed them,
to them (and their safety) was proclaimed.

Hi céin béit ós Banba blaid
anmann na mac ar marthain,
is scél fír fri sílad sin,
ní tic díbad dia daínib.

Long enduring fame over Banba 's renown
as long as the names of her sons endure,
the true story from there is spread,
no quenching will come to her people.

In cnoc in rohailed úag
do mnaí na n-airer n-adúar,
dar cach sogairm suí sana
is dó is togairm tuí Tlachtga. T.

The grave-mound was dug on the hill
of the woman of the very-cold region
among every high-name of a lucky sage
is the high-name of silent Tlachtga.

Tech Duinn
The House of Donn

The House of Donn, Tech Duinn, is where myth tells us the dead go when they first die. There are different versions of how Donn, the first human to die in Ireland, met his end (an alternate version can be found in chapter 5) and took on the role of ruler of Tech Duinn but this is the place name story that includes the most detail and describes the dead going there. It is also worth noting that while Donn is specified to be human in these myths he has taken on the role of a God since then and is also often understood or named as a king among the sidhe in folklore, making him a complex figure. The Irish text is taken for Irish text from Gwynn's Metrical Dindshenchas

---

Teach nDuind, cidh diatá? Ní ansa. In tan dolotar meic Miled aniar don Erinn, asbert a n-druí fríu: 'Fear raghas isin crand siúil', for se, 'Ocus madh é chanus ar tus dichedla for Tuathaib Dei, maighfidh in cath forro, ocus lindi íarsin co brath a tír: ocus bebais in fer cuirfes in m-bricht.'

The house of Donn, what origin? Not difficult. When the sons of Mil came from the west to Ireland, their Druid said to them, "A man must go up that mast ", said he, "and then chant his best druidic chants on the Tuatha De, this will rout the battle on them, and after that time this will be our land forever: and the man will die who casts the spell."

Fochres crandchor forro, ocus tachraidh do Dhonn taidhecht isin seól. Dogníther íarom samlaid, ocus luidh Dond isin seól, ocus canaidh tinchetla fríu, ocus doluidh sís iarsin, ocus asbert: 'Tonga na deo' ol sé, 'cona didhemthar cert no cóir duib festa.'

They set a casting of lots on them, and it was cast to Donn to go to the sail. Afterwards it was done thus, and Donn moved to the sail, and chanted Druidic spells against them, and returned down after, and said: "I swear by the Gods" said he, "we will be without granting justice or recompense to you henceforth."

Canaid-seom dano di thír tinchedla forro-som dia fregra. Iar mallachadh Duinn íarom do Thuaith De dofáinic crith-ghalar fo chétóir isin luing.

They chanted also from the land Druidic spells against them in response. Then they cursed Donn and afterwards the Tuatha De brought a shaking-sickness immediately on the ship.

Asbert Amarghen: 'Bidh marb Dond', for se, 'ocus ní seghdha dund congbail im athgabail an ghalair. Ar día ructhar Dond i tír, bíaidh an galar-sa co brath a n-Erinn.'

Said Amergin, "Donn shall die", said he, "and not lucky his keeping on account of taking back the illness. If we carry Donn to the land, the sickness will be in Ireland forever."

Asbert Dond: 'Berar mo choland-sa', for sé, 'a n-oen na n-ínnsi, ocus dobéra mo chinél bendachtain form co brath.'

Ticc íarom ainbhtine doibh tria thinchedlaibh na n-drúadh, ocus báiter an bárc a m-bái Dond.

Said Donn, "Take my body", said he, "to one of the islands, and my people will give blessing on me forever."

Afterwards through the spell casting of the Druids a storm was brought on them, and the ship of Donn was sunk.

'Berar a choland isin carraic n-aird thall', ol Aimhirghen: conidh de dogarar Teach nDuind. 'Ticfad a munnter an maighin sin', ol Amhirghen.

"Take his body there to that high rock yonder", said Amergin: it will be called Tech Duinn. "His people will go to that place there", said Amergin.

Is aire sin adellad na h-anmanda peccacha co teach nDuind ría techt a n-ifearn, do reír na ngennti, cédus, co tabraid a m-bendachtain for anmain Duinn. Madh anum fírén imorro fir aithrighe is di chéin adcísidhe, ocus ní berar fordul. As i sin tra cédfaidh na ngénnti. Conid desin dogarar Tech nDuind.

And for that burden the souls of sinners visit Tech Duinn before they go to Hell, according to the heathens, indeed, to give their blessings on the soul of Donn. Nevertheless, righteous souls, that is penitent men, they see it from a distance, and do not take a detour there. That is then the opinion of the heathens. So it is called Tech Duinn.

Chapter 4

The Fenian Cycle

I admit that I have the least personal interest in the cycle of myths that focus on the Fianna and their leader Finn mac Cumhaill, so this chapter includes only two pieces. The Fenian cycle is important in the wider range of mythology and does contain many interesting stories, particularly of the Aos sidhe who Fionn has more than one encounter with.

Di Chetharslicht Athgabála
The Four-Regulations of Impounding Property

A story which includes the use of several druidic or magical means of gaining information, known as imbas forosnai and dichetal dochenaib. It is of note in particular for that and for the brief descriptions of their methodology and use. The Irish was found in Meyer's 1904 Revue Celtique article.

Fo chosmailius dorigne Finn húa Baiscne. In tan búi in fian oc Badamair for brú Siúire dodechaidh Cúldub mac húi Birgge a síd ar Femun ut Scotti dicunt co mbert a fulacht núadaib. Co teóra aidchi amin degéni friu. Isin tres fecht iarum norat Finn co luid riam i síd ar Femun. Fortngaib Finn la techt isa síd co torchair allda anall. A ndosreng fris a láim fritninnle in ben asin tsíd & escra fliuch ina láim iar ndáil isin úair riam & doinsort a comlaid frisa síd co ndruid Finn a mér itir in comlaid & in ursain. Gabais iarom a mér ina béolu. Adonic as afrithisi foopairt dicetal. Fortnosmen an imbas condebert: "Tair Femen fuigial formuig meis mui muic cetson sirchrand sirlúath laith find sra aulad Cúlduib chanmae."

Then when the Fian were at Badamair near the border of the Siúire, there emerged Cúldub son of Ûi Birgge from the sídhe of Femun (as the Scots say) and he carried off their cooking. For three nights he did this to them. That third time afterwards Finn went before him to the sídhe of Femun. Finn forcibly seized him as he went into the sídhe and he fell wildly there. He drew back his hand and encountered the woman from the sídhe with a full water vessel in her hands who had been distributing from it and she jammed the door against the sidhe and between the door and doorpost Finn thrust his finger. He thrust his finger into his mouth. Then he began to chant an incantation. Illuminated by the imbas he spoke. "Before Femen evil judgement forms my sow, first-good-omen, longlasting-tree, longlasting-swiftness, shining sovereignty against tomb of Cúlduib I sing"

Cinn ree iarom dobertatar mná braite a Dún Iascaich a tír na nDésea. Dobreth ingen álainn léo. Atecoboride menma Find in ben dó. Focairdd sí menmain for in gilla búi léo .i. Dercc Corra mac húi Daigre. Ar ba hé a abras-side. Céin fonnuithea fulacht léo léim & doléim in gilla tarsin n-indiu. Tre sin didiu carais an ingen é & asbert fris laa n-aill ara tísed cuice i lighe. Ní foét són Dercc Corra déag Finn. Atagegai domnid dó. Cotsáid fri Finn & asbert: "Fortaprom ar écin!"

Asbert iarum Finn fris: "Éirgg es", ol sé, "de m' inchaib & rotbia essomon trí laithi & teóra n-aidchi & fomcialta-sa ó suidhiu inund!"

A time later they carried off captive women from Dún Iascaich from the land of the Désea. A beautiful girl was carried off by them. The mind of Fionn desired the woman for himself. [however] Love was in her mind for the servant they had, that is Dercc Corra son of úi Daigre. This was his habit. Always when they were cooking he would leap and leap back, the servant there every day. For this reason the girl loved him and said to him one day that he should lie down with her. Dercc Corra wouldn't consent to this because of fondness for Finn. She desired vengeance against him. She incited Finn against him and said: "He raped me!"

Then Finn said to him: "Go", he said, "and get out of my sight and you shall have a truce of three days and three nights then be on guard in your seat just the same!"

Luid didiu Derc Corra for loinges & arfoét caill & imtighed for luirgnib oss n-allta (si uerum est) ar a étrumai. Laa n-aill didiu do Find isin caill oc a cuingidh-som co n-aca Find in fer i n-úachtar in craind & lon for a gúalainn ndeis & find-lestar n-uma for a láimh clí, osé co n-usce & hé brecc bedcach and & dam allaith fo bun in craind & ba hé abras ind fir teinm cnó & dobered leth n-airne na cnó don lun nobíth for a gúalaind ndeis, no-ithed feisin al-leth n-aill & doicsed a uball asin lestar n-uma búi for a láimh clí & norandad i ndé & docuireth a leth don dam allaid búi fo bun in craind. No-ithad som iarom in leth n-aill & no-ibed loim fair den uisce asin lestur huma búi for a láim co mbo comól dó frisin n-iich & a n-oss & in lon. Friscomarcar didiu a muinter do Finn cia bo hé hisin crunn, ar nínathgéntar som dáigh celtair díclithe búi imbe.

Then Derc Corra went under banishment and lived in a wood and went on shin-bones of wild deer (if that is true) by his lightness. One day then Finn was there in the wood seeking him when Finn saw a man in the top of a tree and a blackbird beside him on the right and a white-vessel of metal in his left hand, and with a fish and he a leaping trout and a wild stag at the base of the tree and this the action of the man breaking open nuts and he would give half the kernel of the nut to the blackbird eating on his right side, he himself would eat the other half and he would take an apple from the metal vessel in his left hand and divide it in two and give half to the wild stag at the base of the tree. He would eat the other half afterwards and drink the water from the metal vessel that was in his hand so that they feasted together then, the fish the deer and the blackbird. His followers questioned Finn then about who was in the tree, because they didn't recognize him because of the concealment concealing him.

Is de dobert Finn a hordain ina béolo. Addonich as eisib afrithisi fortnosna a imbus & dichan dicetal co n?eipert: 'Con fri lon lethcno contethain cotith in dithraib Dercc Corra comól fri hich ni ba filliud fabaill a uball fín mblais cona fricarbaith mac úi co dedail Daigre.' 'Dercc Corra mac húi Daigre', ol sé, 'fil isan crund'.

So then Fionn placed his thumb in his mouth. He is illuminated as he bites and he begins to chant imbas and dichan dicetal saying: "With a blackbird a half nut vanishes(?) circles(?) the wilderness Dercc Corra agreement of eating turns his course his apple fair tasting against sharp teeth son of úi Daigre."

"Dercc Corra son of úi Daigre", he said, "there in the tree".

Dunaire Fionn

A poem which, despite the name, is a conversation between two heroes of the Fianna, Caoilte and Oisin, over the origin and owners of the Crane Bag, a magical pouch that was made from the skin of a goddess and is used to hold various magical items. The Irish was transcribed from McNeil and Murphy's 1908 text.

VIII

Ceird agam ort Cháoilte, a fir na n-árm n-iomláoite cía ga raipe in Corrbholg cóir, do bhoí ag Cumhall mac Trénmhóir.

A question to you from me Cáoilte, oh man of the exchanged weapons: who has had the well-proportioned Crane-bag, which Cumhall son of Trénmhóir , possessed?

Corr do bhoí ag Manannán mín, fa sed ilbhúadhach go mbrígh día croicionn sin coinndealb borb, de do righnedh in Corrbholg.

A crane it was of gentle Manannán, a treasure of many outstanding qualities of magic-power, a goddess's skin this rough form, from it was made the Crane-bag.

Innis duinne cred in chorr, a Caoilte go n-iolar nglond nó cred far cuiredh a fhir, a croicionn fana sédaib.

Speak to the people, what was the crane, oh Caoilte of many feats, or why was it placed, oh man, her skin about the treasures?

Áiffe ingen Dealbhaoíth dhil, lennan Ilbric oilchrothaigh tarrla for seirc in fhir hí.

Áiofe daughter of beloved Dealbeth, lover of Ilbric of many-beauties; there was love for the man on her and Iuchra of the beautiful complexion.

Agus luchra go gcáoimhlí Cealguis lúchra chum snámha. Aiffe nocar chuairt ágha dan cuir hí tré luinne amoigh. A riocht cuirre fo chuirrchib.

Iúchra tricked Aíofe into going swimming with her. No valorous visit was this visit; she chased her fiercely away from there in the shape of a crane through marshes.

Fíefraighis Aoíffe íer sin. D'ingin áuinn Ábhartaigh ga fad bhíad sa riocht so a bhen, a luchra álionn uichtgheal.

Aoífe then asked her this. "Beautiful daughter of Ábhartaigh for how long will I live in this form oh, woman, oh fair luchra bright-bosomed?"

An críoch chuirfet ní bag err, ort a Aoíffe na rosc ró-mhall beir-si da ched blíadhuin bán, a ttigh mhíadhaigh Mhanannán.

"The end will not be short on you oh Aoífe of the gentle eyes, you will be two hundred white years in the noble house of Manannán."

Bíaidh tú sa tigh sin do gnáth, ag fanamhat fút do chách ad chuirr nach dtaisdil gach tír, noch attacfainn tú entír.

"You shall be always in the house there with the common people jeering long at you all the time, a crane not travelling each land, you shall not reach any land."

Do ghentor sioghtheach maith réd, dot croicionn ní beg in béd bidh é a ainm sní bréag dhamh Corrbholg na réd fo dheireadh.

"A fairy-house of good things will become of your skin, not a small occurance, it's name, without lie the things I've said, Crane-bag in time."

Do rinne Manannán sin, do croicionn od fúair oighidh do bhí fo gach réd dhíobh sin, aige ni breg na deghaidh.

Manannán made this of her skin after she was killed to keep every thing he would there, that time, no lie, afterwards.

Léine Mhanannáin sa sgein, is crios Goibhnionn ar áon-ríen duphán gabhann ón fhior bhorb, seóid do bhíod issin Chorrbholg.

Manannán's shirt and knife, the corslet of Goibhnionn in harmony, a smith-hook loaned [from] a fierce man. Treasures held by the Crane-bag.

Deimhios righ Alban gan fheall, agus cathbharr ríogh lochlann do bhoí ann re ráite sin, agus cnamha muc nAsail.

The King of Scotland's shears, without deceit, and the King of Norway's helmet were there as we tell this, and the bones of Asail's swine.

Crios do dhruimnibh an míl móir, do bhoí sa Corrbholg choir ader-sa riot gan dochar, do bhiodh ann ga iomachar.

A corslet of the spine of the whale, was in the well-proportioned Crane-bag I tell you truly, it was there carried in it.

In tan do bhíod in muir lán, ba follur a hseóid ar a lár inuair fa tráigh in muir borb, folamh fo deóidh in Corrbholg.

When it was full-sea the treasures bulged at the surface and when the rough-sea was at ebb-tide it was empty in succession, the Crane-bag.

Ag sin duit a Oissín fhéil, mar do ríghnedh é budhdéin agus inneosad fesda, a imthur a himtechta.

There it is to you Oisín yourself, how it was created the same, and I shall tell now, its goings, its wanderings.

Ro bhoí in Corrbholg ré fada, ag Lugh láochda Lamh-fada no gur thuitin ríg fo dheóidh, le macaibh Cearmada Milbheóil do bhí in Corrbholg eir sin, aca sin ina deghoidh.

The Crane-bag for a long time after was with heroic Lugh of the Long Arm until finally the king was killed by the sons of Cermad Milbheóil

Gur thuitsiod in tríar germ ear, lé macaibh móra Míledh.

It remained there with them, until they were killed, although the three were nobly keen, by the sons of great Míl.

Tainic Manannán gan sgís. rucc leis in Corrbholg arís níor taisbéin é do dhuine. go ttainic ré Conaire.

Manannán came without fatigue. He carried off the Crane-bag once again without showing it to any person, until the time of Conaire arrived.

Ro codail Conaire cáomh, do leathtaoibh Temhrach na ráon mar do musgail in glan glic, frith in Corrbholg fá braguit. Etc.,

Fair Conaire slept on the side of Tara of the paths thus he woke, the pure clever one, the Crane-bag was found around his neck. Etc.,

Chapter 5

Miscellaneous

This chapter contains a variety of short pieces which don't fit in well elsewhere. Some of them, like the first piece, are from a different mythic cycle which I don't have enough material to do an entire chapter on while others are taken from assorted sources that don't belong properly to any of the cycles. The material here covers more cohesive tales as well as snippets of material focusing on magical charms, holidays, and gods.

Apraid a éolchu Elga
By Eochaid Eolach ua Céirín

> This text is, to my knowledge, not publicly available anywhere in English outside of my own translation. It contains some interesting and important information about various figures and members of the Tuatha De Danann. Irish text transcribed from Thurneyesen's 1896 article in Zeitschrift für celtische Philologie.

Duan in chethrachat cest in so, do-rigni Eochaid ua Cérín
Apraid a éolchu Elga
a slúaig Fótla fírergna.
in-fetabair thiar no thair.
ainm mná Féniusa Fárrsaid?
Bélait ingen Laitin máthair Níuil meic Féniusa.
Gae greíne rus-marb.

The poem of the forty questions by Eochaid
Speak, you knowledgeable Irish

host of the truly famous Ireland,
do you know in the west or east
the name of the wife of Fénius Farsaid?
Bélait the daughter of Laiten, mother of Nél son of Fénius Farsaid.
A ray of sunshine killed her.

Cía fer ro-marb Iár na n-each.
cia h-airmm 'sa-fríth a airlech
ni bás ro-fuc cíar-gegain.
int éoluch co n- ilbérlaib
.i. Féinius féin ro-marb Iar mac Néma
do leccain chámaill íar n-dula do Iar co Bélait
& marb Bélait do grád & ro-adhnocht h-i Carnn Bélaite.

Which man killed Iar of the horses?
What place was his slaying?
Death did not take him dark-branched,
the knowledgeable with the many languages.
That is Fénius himself killed Iar son of Néma
with the jaw of a camel after Iar went to Bélait,
and Bélait died of love and was buried in Carn Bélaite.

Cía h-aiged rucc Feínius feín.
i focus i n-eterchein?
c' áitt ro-adnacht in suí sean.
Iar macc Nému na nainteam?
.i. marb Féinius dana íar .u. láib do digh dermuit
coro-adnacht h-i tuaiscirt Maigi Senair
.i. in Eipithena ciuitate ro-adnocht Iar
& nir-léc Féinius a adhnocul fein & Iar maróen i n-óencathair.

Which violent death took Fénius himself,
near or far?

Where is the grave of the old sage
Iar mac Néma of ( )?
That is Fénius also died after 5 days of drinking a great amount
and was buried in the north of the plain of Senar.
That is in the city of Epithena Iar was buried
and Fénius did not allow himself to be buried with Iar together in the same city.

Is cuich in triar tairptech teann.
ro-buí d' eísi na díleann.
co-failet a beinn i m-beinn.
as cach dithrib i nh-Érinn?
.i. tri bráthri do Chessair táncatar h-Érinn áenagaig ría n-dílinn
& niro-acaillsit itir Cessair.
Luám & Medar & Mel a n-anmann,
i n-delbuib eón ro-bátar & i m-Beinn Bairche ro-bátar.

And who are the violent, strong three
who lived after the flood,
so that they are from peak to peak
over every wilderness in Ireland?
That is three brothers of Cessair came to Ireland the night before the flood
and did not speak to Cessair.
Luam and Medar and Mel were their names
They were in the shape of birds and they were on Benn Boirche.

Cid thuc Partholón ó thír.
cid ara-nderna mórgním?
Cía lín ro-buí a glinn i n-glinn.
cid arro-díth a n-Érinn?
.i. Parttolón ro-marb a athair & a máthair

ac íarair ríghe dia bráthair
(conid aire at-berar Parrtolón mac Sera friss .i. mac fingalach. cera .i. fingal),
co-tánicc co h-Érinn ar teched a finghaile,
conid íarum luid taimlechta ina fingail .i. .ix. m. do éc fri oínsechtmain díb.

What took Partholón out of his country?
Why did he do the great deed?
How many was he with from valley to valley?
Where did he die in Ireland?
That is Partholón killed his father and his mother,
because he wanted the kingship for his brother
(with noble named Partholon son of Sera that is son of Fingalach. Cera that is Fingal)
And he came to Ireland fleeing his kinslaying.
Afterwards came a plague for his kinslaying: 9000 of them died in one week

Cía ro-buí for Temraig.
diar-fear snechta airdergnaid?
In rann ro-buí a Temraig de.
ba h-argat fíal findruine.
.i. h-i sechtmad blíadain flatha Éna Aircthig ro-fer froiss airget h-i Temruig
& fross fína for h-Érinn uile.

Which ruled at Temair
when the noble snow fell?
The part of it that fell on Temair
was fine silver electrum.
That is in the seventh year of Éna Airgtech's reign, a rain of silver fell in Temair
and a rain of wine fell over all Ireland.

Coich in maccóem co mét n-glonn.
ránic Eamuin cin imroll.
ro-marb deich cét monar n-glé.
dia muinntir i n-oénaidque?
.i. Aengus dana mac In Dágda is é ránicc Emuin
ar bréthir Concobair dia-n-epert: 'for-ossna Cú Chulainn cach óen.'
& ro-marb Oengus .x.c. isin Cráebrúaid & ro-chuimrig Coin Culainn
& do-fuc Conall & Celtchair & Conchobor h-i suán.

Who is the young man of great deeds
who came to Emain without error
He killed a thousand, a clear task,
people in one night?
That is skilled Oengus, the son of the Dagda, came to Emain
because of the words of Conchobor when he said: 'CuChulainn outshines everyone.'
And Oengus killed a thousand in Craebruad and bound Cú Chulainn
and put Conall and Celtchair and Conchobor to sleep

Cía dalta dia daltaib thair.
ro-sáraigustar Etain?
ocus abair rimm co glicc.
cade ainm athur Seinbicc?
.i. Abcán ua h-Ebricc in file is é
ro-sáruigh Etan ingean Dián Cécht at brú Boínne
gu rus-toirrchiustur,
co-toracht Oengus iar sain gurro-marb Abcán.
Conid íarum ruc Etan Senbec & Oengus ro-n-alt Senbeciar sin.

Which foster son of his foster sons in the east
raped Etan?
And tell it to me shrewdly:
what is the name of Senbec's father?

That is Abcán grandson of Ebricc the poet is he
who raped Etan daughter of Dian Cécht on the bank of the Boyne River
and impregnated her.
Then Oengus came there separately and killed Abcán.
Then Etan brought Senbec and Oengus raised Senbec there.

Anmonn na trí son n-doilbthe.
na-fácbaid co anforbthi.
.i. Gó dana & anfír & ainfiss a n-anmonn na sonndoilbthe.
cid fod-era sund co se
soillse 'sin chrunn is brénche?
.i. diaro-eírig Críst asa adnocul is ed ro-chét saltair for crann crín, ut est tene sinnuig.

The names of the three with the false appearance,
do not leave them incomplete.
That is skilled Gó and Anfír and Ainfiss are the names of the violent-appearing.
What is the effect on him
The glow there in the tree, the decay?
That is when Christ rose from his grave, he sang the psalter over a decayed trunk, hence the 'will o the wisp'

Cía do-rigni gart ar tús.
in-fetabair a imthús?
.i. Seth mac Ádaim do-rat fleid dia bráthrib h-i Sléib Taboir
& tuc crod da cach bráthair díb,
co-farcaibsit bennachtain
oca searb ocus milis molle.
cid dos-fucc i nd-oénoidque
.i. Míchél at-bert fri Ádam: bennach lat na torthi, ar dot-roa demon aslaigh iterum dot malairt im no toirthi.
Cach ní no-bennach Ádam is miliss, cach ní tárill demon is serb.

Who showed hospitality first?
Do you know his history?
That is Seth son of Adam gave a feast to his brothers on Mount Tabor
and gave cattle to each brother among them
so that they might leave him their blessing.
With bitter and sweet at the same time,
what did it create in one night?
That is Michael said to Adam: 'Bless the fruits; for the tempting demon will come to you again to destroy you or else the fruits. Everything that Adam blessed is sweet; everything the devil got is bitter.

Cía do rígraidib Fer m-Bolc.
ro-gab Érinn cíarb anord
i m-Maigh Tured trúagh in dáil.
tuc cath do Túaith Dé dámaigh.
.i. Tríath mac Amuir in rí deídenoch do Feruib Bolg in nómad rí díb.
Ocus is h-é tuc cath Maighe Turead do Thúathaib Dé Danonn.

Which of the kings of the Fir Bolg,
who ruled Ireland (with) bad leadership,
on Mag Tured, wretched the meeting,
gave battle with the retinue of the Tuath Dé?
That is Triath son of Amuir, the last king of the Fir Bolg, was the ninth king among them.
And he gave battle at Mag Tured to the Tuatha Dé Danann.

Cadead anmunn na sé m-ban.
& anmunn a n-athar.
tucsat léo Meic Míled muáid.
o Thúaith Dé Danann drechruáid?
.i. Lían & Liphi & Lemain tri h-ingena Midir.
Aillenn & Cuilleann & Cairchi .iii. ingena Goibnenn.

What are the names of the six women
and the names of their fathers
who took the sons of the noble Mil
from the red-faced Tuath Dé Danann?
That is Lian and Liphe and Lemain, Mider's three daughters.
Aillenn and Cuillenn and Cairche, the three daughters of Goibniu.

Ocus anmunn na fear trá.
cusa-ndeachatar na mná.
a aés dána na n-dúan dil.
éistigh uán ocus apraidh.
.i. Lían co Cuáilgne,
Lifi co Fúat,
Lemain co Murthemni,
Aillenn co Lugaidh,
Cuillenn co Surghe,
Cairche ra Sobairche.

And the names of the men then
to whom the women came:
people of art with the beloved poems,
listen to us and speak.
That is Lian to Cuailgne,
Life to Fuat,
Lemain to Murthemne,
Aillenn to Lugaid,
Cuillenn to Surge,
Cairche to Sobairche.

Cía rí díb déighenach dián.
ro-gab for gasrad Gaílían?
ocus apraid rimm cen ail.
cía ainm boí forsin rígh-sain?
.i. tri rí déc díb ó Thúathaib Dé Danann for h-Érinn co-táncatar Meic Miled

.i. Gola ó-sluinnter Slíab n-Gola h-i Ciaraighe is é ba rí déigenach díb.

Which swift, final king among them
had the warriors of the Gailian?
And tell me without reproach
what name was on this king?
That is thirteen kings of the Tuatha Dé Danann ruled Ireland until the sons of Miled came.
That is Gola, after whom Sliab n-Gola is named in Kerry, who was the last king of them.

Ocus ainm mná Ébir aird.
ni-fetatar na doérbaird.
ainm a máthar cemafath.
ocus ainm a degathar.
.i. Adair dana ingen In Dagda móir
is í ro-faei la h-Éber
.i. in Mórrigan dana ainm a m-máthar Adairi mná Ébir.

And the name of the noble Éber's wife
the base poets do not know him
the name of her mother (?)
and the name of her noble father.
That is Adair the daughter of the great Dagda,
who cohabited with Éber;
That is the skilled Morrígan is the name of the mother of Adair wife of Eber.

Caide a n-díl ó sin alle.
Túaithe Dé na trommdaíne.
innisid abus is tair.
caide a n-ord ocus apraidh.
Apraid a eol-.

What is their fate from then until now,
the powerful people of the Tuatha De?
Proclaim it at here and in the east,
what is their honour, and speak
Speak wisely

Compert Mongan
The Conception of Mongan

The story of how Manannán mac Lir travelled to the human world in order to father an important hero and king. As with several other pieces in this book the Irish text is only a partial one and so I have included summaries of the missing material for context. Irish from the Lebor na hUidre

---

(Fiachna is off fighting in Scotland when a noble-looking stranger appears to his wife at home and asks her for a meeting between them. She refuses saying she would not disgrace her husband; the stranger asks if she would tryst with him to save her husband's life and she replies that she would do anything in her power to save him if she could)

Asbertsa dagní didiu "ar atá do chéle i ngúais már. Tucad fer húathmar ara chend nad forsabatár & atbéla leis. Dia ndernam mád tú caratrad berae mac de. Bid amre in mac bid Fíacnai dano. Regasa dun chath firfidir i mbárach im theirt aranícubsa & fessa in mílid ar bélaib fer nAlban. & asbert frit chéliusiu ar n-imtechta & as tussu rom foídi día chobair."

Dogníth samlaid.

[text picks up after gap]

He said that she should do it then because "your husband is in great danger. A terrible man goes against him and he will die by him. If you have a [sexual] alliance with me a son will come from it. Famous will be the son of Fíachna. I will go to the battle in the third hour tomorrow and it will be told by all the mouths of the men of Scotland. And I will tell your husband of these wanderings and that you sent help to him."

It was done.

In tan reras in cath díarailiu co n-accatar ní in tslúaig in fer sainigthe ar beolo catho Áedain & Fiachna. Dolluid dochum Fiachna in tainredach & asbert fris accaldaim a mná a llá ríam & donindgell dia chobair isind uair sin. Luid iarom resin cath dochum alaili & fich in mílid & memuid in cath ria nÁedán & Fiachna

When they went into the battle the gathered hosts saw the man and the warriors of Áedain and Fiachna whispered of him. He went to Fiachna in particular and spoke of the discussion with his wife before and that he had promised to give his help in that hour. Then he went and fought against the others and vanquished the soldiers and the battle was won by Áedán and Fiachna.

& dointaí Fíachna día chrích & bá torrach in ben .i. ben & birt mac .i. Mongan mac Fíachna & atlugestar a céli a ndogéni friss & addámirsi a imthechta uli. Conid mac do Manannán mac Lir intí Mongán césu Mongan mac Fiachnai dogarar dé. ar foracaib rand lía máthair a llude uadi matin a n-asbert Tíag dum daim dufail in matin bánglain iss é Monindan mac Lir ainm ind fir dutárlid.

And Fiachna went back to his country and the woman was pregnant, that is the woman gave birth to a son, that is Mongan mac Fíachna and he thanked his wife for what she had done and she told all her adventures to him. He was a son of Manannán mac Lir this Mongán though Mongan mac Fiachna was the name on him. When the man went from [Mongan's] mother he left this poem which he said to her in the morning:

I go to my house,
the clear-bright morning is at hand,
it is he Manannán mac Lir,
the name of the man who came to you.

Tri Cuirn o Cormac ua Cuinn
The Three Goblets[84] of Cormac Ua Cuinn

A tale of three magical goblets. The Irish text is from RIA MS 23 O 48: Liber Flavus Fergusiorum, 1435–40

Feacht n-ann do luid Aedh Oirdnidhi mac Neill Frosaidh mic Fearghuile mic Maile Duin do ordugud fer cuigid Connacht. Do luid dar Eas Ruaidh ocus do baithed a fuis meisi ocus a cuirnn ann. Tainic Aedh co riacht Corca Tri, co n-deisidh a tigh righ Corca Tri. Coeca righ do riguibh Eirenn maille re h-Aedh.

There was one time Aed Oridnide, son of Nial Frosach, son of Feargal, son of Maelduin, came to bring order to the men of the province of Connacht. He went over Eas Ruaid and his table-attendants and his goblets drown there. Aed went until he reached Corca Tri, and rested at the house of the king of Corca Tri. Fifty kings of the kings of Ireland were along with Aed.

Longuis Aedh adhaigh domhnaidh ocus an rigraidh: ocus cia ro loing Aed, ni sib digh, uair ní bai corn lais, or do baitheadh a cuirnn ocus a cuaich ac Ath Enaigh uas Eas Ruaidh, oc tiachtain don t-sluadh thairis. As amal immoro robai Aed cona sibh digh a leastur aile o ra dealuigh re cich a mathar acht a curn. Ba bron tra do righ Corca Tri ocus dia seithid, each ic ol ocus righ Erenn gin ol. Togbuis Angal a lamha fri Dia, ocus feicis gin codladh gin tomailt co madain.

Aed ate on Sunday night and the kings [as well]: but though he ate he drank no drink, because he had no goblet, because his goblets and his cups were submerged at Ath Enaig, above Eas Ruaid, as the army was taking it. It was thus around Aed with them drinking from other vessels of great distinction as if from the breast of their mother but his goblet alone [was missing].

It was a sadness for the king of Corca Tri and his wife that the horse nearby was drinking and the king of Ireland without drinking. Angal raised his hands to God, and went on without sleep [and] without food until morning.

Gu n-eabert a bean fris ara barach, 'Eirg,' ar si, 'co Dirlus Guaire mic Colmain, uair ba tealach feile ocus naire o aimsir Dathi anall, dus an fuigbithea corn tria firta na feile ann.'

The next day his wife said to him: "Go," said she, "to Dirlus, to Guaire son of Colmain , for that has been the house of welcome and generosity from the time of Dathi on, to see if you would get a goblet there through his wonderful generosity."

Cechaing Angal righ Corca Tri tar dorus na ratha amach, ocus tuisleas a cois deas, co ra tuisil cloch leis isin lis .i. an cloch do bai ar belaib an t-suirn a rabudar na tri cuirn as deach robai a n-Eirinn .i. an Cam-corn ocus an Litan ocus an Easgung. Cuirn sin tucad do Cormac u Cuinn dar muir, ocus ro folaig Niamh mac Lugna Firtri an dara comalta do Cormac u Cuinn, iar n-dith Cormuic, co toracht Coirpri Lifeachuir dar muir ocus cia ro fritha na cuirn aile la Cairpri, ni fritha na cuirn-siu co h-aimsir na næmh ocus Aeda Oirdnidi mic Neill, or tucad cealtar tairsib o Dia, co ru-s-foillsid do righ Corca Tri tria firta na feile.

Angal, king of Corca Tri, proceeded through the door of the fort outwards, and his right foot slipped, and a stone fell from the fort that is the stone that covered the mouth of the division where were the three goblets that were best in Ireland that is the Curved-Horn, and the Litany, and the Eel. These were the goblets that were brought by Cormac grandson of Conn over the sea; and they were hidden by Niamh son of Lugna Firtri, the second foster-brother of Cormac grandson of Conn, after the slaughter of Cormac; and Cairpri Lifeachuir came over the sea, and though the other goblets were found by Cairpri, these goblets were not found till the time of the saints and of Aed Oridnide son of Nial. Because a cloak went to cover them of God, until they were revealed to the king of Corca Tri, through his wonderful generosity.

Altaigis a buidi do dia an t-i Angal ocus beiris leis na curna, cona tri lan do mid inntibh. Do-bert a laim Aeda Oirdnidi righ Eirenn, ocus atlaigi do dia ocus do-bert an Litan a laim righ Ulad, ocus do-bert an Easguing a laimh righ Connacht, ocus fagbuis aigi budhein an Cam-cornn.

Angal gave thanks to God, and went with the goblets, with the three full of mead. He put them in the hands of Aed Oirdnide, king of Ireland, who gave thanks to God, and put the Litany in the hands of the king of Ulster, the Eel in the hands of the king of Connacht, and reserved to himself the Curved-Horn.

Co toracht iartain do Mailseachloinn mac Domhnuill, co tuc-sidhe do Dia ocus do Ciaran a coitcinne co brath.

Successively afterwards [it went] to Maelsechlainn son of Domhnaill; it went as a peace-offering to God and to Ciaran, generally, until Judgement.

Imram Brian Meic Ferbail
Excerpt from the Wandering of Bran son of Ferbal

This is not the entire story of the wanderings of Bran but rather a partial text that explains how Bran returned to Ireland and left again after telling his story. Irish text from the Lebor na hUidre

---

[gap: chasm in MS/extent: uncertain]

Lil in chertle dia dernaid boí in snáthe inna certle hi lláim inna mná consreng dochom poirt. Lotar iarom hi tegdais máir arránic imda cach lánamna and .i. tri .ix. n-imdae. In praind dobreth for cach méis nír ircran díib

[begins after gap in text]

The white ball of thread was in his palm, the thread of the ball of thread was in the woman's hand pulling them towards port. Then they went into a large house where they found a bed for every couple there that is three times nine beds. The meal given on every platter was not emptied from them.

Ba bliadain donarfás dóib bith and ecmaing batir ilbliadna ni tesbi cach mblas. Gabais eólcaire fer diib .i. Nechtan mac Collbrain. Atchid a cenel fri Bran ara tía leis dochom nErend. Asbert in ben ropad aithrech in fáboll dálotar cammae. & asbert in ben arná tuinsed nech díb a tír & ara taidlitís léu in fer fodnácaibset i n-Inis na Mell tar essi a chéli.

There was a year's growth to them in that world there but it happened that there were many years with no savour lacking to them. A longing for home took a man of them that is Nechtan son of Collbran. Bran saw his kindred against him that he should go with him to Ireland. The woman said an assault of regret would be the going nevertheless. And the woman said therefore none of them should touch the land and that they visit with the man left in Inis na Mell who they'd left out of their companions.

Dollotár iarom co tornachtatár in dáil hi Srúib Brain. Iarmofochtatarside dóib cía dolluid in muir.

They went afterwards until they came to a gathering at Bran's headland. The men asked who it was that had come across the sea.

Asbert Bran "messe" or se "Bran mac Febail".

Bran answered, "It is me," he said, "Bran son of Ferbal."

"Ni beram achni aní sin" ol a chéli di híu. "Atá i ssenchassaib lenni chena Imram Brain."

"We do not recognize this one" said the others to him. "[but] There are old stories of Bran's Voyage."

Docurethar úadib in fer asin churuch. Amal condránicside fri talmannaib na Herend bá lúathred fó chetóir amal bid hi talom no beth tríasna hilcheta bliadna. Is and cáchain Bran in rand so.

He put himself out, the man [Nechtan], from the coracle. So that as soon as he was against the earth of Ireland he was dust immediately as if he'd been under the earth without life through many years. Then chanted Bran the section following:

Do mac Colbrain ba mór mbaíss
tórgud a láme fri aís
can nech dorratad toind usci glain
tar Nechtan mac Collbrain.

"To the son of Colbrain, was a lack of judgment
Bringing his hand against a lifetime
without conferring any wave of pure water
to Nechtan son of Collbrain."

Adfet iar sin Bran a imthechta uli o thossuch co tici sin do lucht ind airechtais & scribais inn rundnu so tre ogum & celebrais doib iar sin & ní fessa a imthechta ónd úair sin.

Then Bran told of all his wanderings from the start until then to the people gathered there and wrote these sections in Ogham and told them farewell and no one knows his wanderings from that hour.

Fiachairecht - Raven Lore

There's a fascinating bit of text called 'Fiachairecht ocus Dreanacht' or, roughly 'Raven Augury and Wren Augury' that outlines in detail what exactly omens with these birds mean based on where they are when the omen is received. I've decided to divide it up into sections, starting with 'Fiachairecht' (Raven Augury). The Irish text is taken from Best, R.I. *Prognostications from the Raven and the Wren,* Ériu 1916.

FIACHAIRECHT

Madh congaire an fiach os imdha comdluthta a medon an tighe is ardgres liath no chlerig ticc cucad, acht ata deithbir eturru .i. mad laoch clerech is bacach adeir an fiach, madh fer graidh is gradh gradh congair ocus is fo do do ló congair. Madh gresa oclaich no caintidh ticc and is graacc gracc congair, no as grob grob ocus i lleith ad diaigh congair ocus as as tecaid na gressa. Mad gracc gracc congair fordhighthir na hoicc dia ngair. Mad mna tic and is foda congair. Mad congaire don aird aniartuaidh don tigh meirligh ar ti na n-each do ghaid. Mad ar dorus an tighe congair coimighthi no amhuis ticc ann. Mad os dorus congair cainti no gresa do lucht comaitechta righ tic ann. Mad os imda in fir maith congair airm a mbia a gascidh ocus se ac dul for fecht ni ticfa slan ocus minab eadh ticcfa imslan. Madh í in ben nodbebhus is andsan adhart congair. Mad a cosuibh imdha in fir congair ticfa a mac no a brathair no a chliamain don tigh. Mad a forimel na cuiled airm a mbi an biadh inti congair is tormach mbidh don leith asa ngair .i. carna no cetbleghon bo. Madh ider an cuilidh ocus tene a aighidh, aidhigh combind ticc don tigh. Mad nesu do mnai an tighe airm a mbi na suidi it le na greasa .i. cilamuin no cara. Mad fri cuilid andes congair altrum no gresu a céin ticc don tigh. Mad guth bec asberu .i. err err no úr úr galar for nec[h] isin tigh no for ni dia ceathra. Mad coin ticc fona caorchaib as don cru caorach congair no a n-urcomuir na mna maithi ocus is edh adeir carna carna grob grob coin coin. Mad congaire do chleith an tighe an tan bithter ag longud caithid an longud sin. Mad do chloich congair tasc athaigh sin. Mad do chrund ard congair tascc oigtigerna indsin. Madh do chleith in craind tasc rig no meic saorcheneoil. Mad dia ndech leat for feacht no romat ocus mad failidh fair bidh maith do thurus ocus doberthar úrcharna duit. Mad tuathbil dotes ocus congair fort belaib is tru forsa ngair amlaid no fordergadh for neach don foirind. Mad for do belaib ac dul docum dala coimeirghi inti. Mad tuaithbel dodeocha marbthar nech don coimeirghe sin. Mad congaire de chuil na n-each rneirlig fora ti. Mad dia soa foen ocai ocus dia n-abra grob grob gadtar ni dona hechaib ocus ni fuidhbiter ocus rt.

RAVEN LORE

If the raven calls over an enclosed sleeping couch in the middle of the house grey-haired, noble guests or clerics are coming towards you, but there is a difference between them that is if lay-clergy then 'bacach' says the raven, if a man of ecclesiastical orders then 'gradh gradh' it calls and calls so twice a day. If warrior guests or satirists are coming it calls 'graacc gracc', or 'grob grob' and in the grayness of evening calls and the guests are coming. If it calls 'gracc gracc' the youths are suffering for a short time. If women are coming its call is long. If it calls from the north-east point of the house bandits are about to steal the horses. If it calls from a doorway of the house foreigners or hirelings are coming there. If above the doorway it calls satirist or guests in the household attending a king are coming there. If it calls above a sleeping couch of the good man, where his weapons will be, and he ready to go for a time, he will not go safely yet he act gently however he will go in safety. If it is the woman who shall die then from a pillow it calls. If it's from the foot of the man's sleeping couch it calls his son or his brother or his male in-law will come to his house. If it calls from the edge of the storeroom where the food is stored in the food will increase from the part of that quantity, that is meat or first milk-yield of the cow. If its face is between the storehouse and fire, sweet countenances will come to his house. If it calls near to the woman of the house, her usual place, it will be the guests of the aforementioned that is a male in-law or a friend. If it calls toward the right of the storehouse a new foster or long-term guest are coming to the house. If it speaks with a small voice, that is 'err err' or 'úr úr' illness on someone in that house or on something in the herds. If wolves will come among the sheep, it calls from the sheep-stock or the raven calls by the good woman and it says 'carna carna', 'grob grob' 'coin coin' [wolves, wolves]. If it calls from the ridgepole of the house when they are eating their meal they cast away the meal there. If it calls from a stone it is news of a commoner's death there. If he calls in a high tree news of a young lord's death. If from a hidden tree a king or noble's son's death-news. If one go with you on a journey or before you and if happiness is on it [if it is happy] your journey will go well and new meat will be given to you. If it comes lefthand-wise and calls on you, he is doomed who this cry is on thus, or doom on someone in the group. If before you close to going to the assembly, an uprising at the aforementioned. If lefthand-wise it has come a death of someone at the uprising there. If it calls from the horses' corner thieves are about to attack. If it turns over on its back then and it says 'grob grob' some unlucky horses will be stolen and not be found and so on.

Dreanacht - Wren Augury

The second part of the text on raven and wren augury. Original text followed by my translation. The Irish text is taken from Best, R.I. *Prognostications from the Raven and the Wren*, Ériu 1916.

DREANACHT

Mad congaire an ceanandan duit anair turus daine craibtheach cucad co n-agairbe fort. Madh anairdes gaires an drean druith uallcha doroith. Mad aniar esurraidh dobi cucaib. Mad anairtuaidh goires aes lasa mbi cele fesa no mna tic and. Mad atuaidh is inmuin leat anti tic and. Mad aniartuaidh tic aes craibthech tic and. Mad od leith anneas gairesacht minab edrud ocus grian turus inmuin tic cucaib. Mad edrut ocus grian guin duine dil duit no adharc fort budéin. Mad ad cluais cli comrac fri hóg ua cein no fess la mnai óic. Mad ad deaghaidh gaires guidhi do mna d'fer ele dod chind. Mad for talmain tis ad deaghaid berthar do ben uaid ar eigin. Mad anair gaires an drean aes dana do thiachtain cuccad no scela uathaibh. Mad andes id diaigh gaires taisigh clerech maith nodcífi no tasc athlaoch uasul adcluinfe. Mad aniardhes gaires ladraind ocus drochbachlaigh ocus drochmhna do thiachtuin cucad. Mad aniar drochdhaine gail tic ann. Mad aniartuaidh gaires deghlaoch sochenelach ocus brugadha uaisle ocus mná maithi dothic ann. Mad atuaigh gaires drochdaine tic ann, gidhad oig gidhad clerigh cidad drochmna ocus aos ochaid aingidh do rochtain. Mad andes gaires galur no coin allta for do chethruib. Mad do thalmain no do chloich no do chrois gaires tasc duine moir indisis duit. Mad do chrosuib imda gaires ar daine sin ocus in lin fechtus teid forsin talmain is ed in lin marb dlomus, ocus an leth forsa mbi a aghaid is as dlomus na mairb.

WREN AUGURY

If the little fair headed one calls to you from the east people of devotion journey to you with severity on you. If southeast the wren calls false-bearded fools will arrive. If from the southwest, landless men are coming to you. If from the northeast it calls people with entertainment for the night or women are coming there. If from the north one who is beloved to you is he that is coming there. If from the northwest people of devotion are coming there. If it sings from the south side, it calls, although not between you and the sun, a beloved on a journey is coming to you. If it is between you and the sun wounding of a person dear to you or destruction on you yourself. If near the left ear yourself contesting against a young man or sleeping with a young woman. If near the back of you it calls an invitation by your woman to another man following you. If on the ground below near your back your wife will be taken from you indeed. If from the east the wren calls poets are coming to you or news from them. If from the south behind you it calls good, concealed clergy you will see or you will hear death-news of a noble ex-layman. If it calls from the southwest thieves and bad servants and bad women are coming to you. If from the west bad warlike people are coming there. If it calls from the northwest a good warrior from a noble family and noble hospitallers and good women are coming there. If from the north it calls bad people are coming there, or young warriors or clerics or bad women and cruel inciting people will be arriving. If it calls from the south illness or wild wolves on your herds. If from the ground or from a stone or from cross it calls death news of great people it announces to you. If from many crosses it calls it is a slaughter of men and the full number it journeys between there and the earth is the full count of the dead it proclaims, and they will be from the side on which it faces as it proclaims the dead

Tech Duinn
House of Donn

A short excerpt from the Lebor Gabala Erenn which offers a different understanding of how Donn died and how Tech Duinn came to be. The Irish text is taken from the *Lebor Gabala Erenn*

Atbert Dond. "Dobersa" ar se "fo gin gai ocus chlaidib innossa na fail i nHerind."

Ocus deligis in gaeth friu in luing i mbai Dond & Herech da mac Miled & in luing i mbaí Bress & Búas & Buagne. Coro baitte ocna Dumachaib oc Taig Duind. Duma cach fir and.

Donn said, "I will bring" said he, "under edge of spear and sword now the land of Ireland."

And the wind separated against him [and] the ship of Donn and Herech, two sons of Mil, and the ship of Bress and Búas and Buagne. They were thrown; they drown close to Dumachaib at Tech Duinn. The grave-mound of every man is there.

Excerpts from Cóir Anmann

The Cóir Anmann or 'Rightness of Names' is a text which lists an array of figures across mythology and pseudo-history and includes brief descriptions of each. For this portion I have focused on verses 149 through 157 which feature several of the Tuatha De Danann. These descriptions are important and give us insight into how these beings were understood between the 11th and 13th centuries in Ireland when the text was written. The Irish text is from Stokes (1887) Irische Texte mit Übersetzugen und Wörterbuch

---

149 *Tuatha Dea (.i. Donann) .i. dée in t-áes dána & andeé in t-áes trebhtha; amail asrubhairt Cú .cc. for Taín Bó Cúailnge, día m-bái a toirrsi & a n-ítaidh mhóir déis Lóich meic Mofeidbis do mharbad. INtan bói Cú Chulainn isin comrag sin Lóich, taínic chuigi In Mhórríghan inghen Ernmhais a richt anaichnidh a sidhibh do bhasgadh Con Culainn isin comhrag. Tug Cú Chulainn root n-urchuir donMhórrighain gura bhris a lethrosc. Taínic sí aridhisi a richt t-seantainne d'innsaighi Chon Culainn, & dobhí sí ag bleghan bó tri sine ina fiadhnaisi. IS ime tra táinic sí arbíthin a foírithnech do Choin Culainn, daigh ní ghonadh Cú Chulainn nech araterná[d] co m-beth cuid dó fein ina leighis. Conaitecht Cú Chulainn in bleóghan fuirri iarna dhéchradh d'ítaidh. Dobreth sí blegan sine dó. 'Rob slán an neim damh-sa só!' ar Cú Chulainn. Bá slán didiu lethrosc na ríghna annsin. Ar Cú Chulainn robhris a lethrosc roime sin. Conaitecht som bleoghan sine aile fuirri. Dobert sí dó. 'An neimh rob slán intí doridhnacht', or Cú Chulainn. Conatach som in tres n-digh & dobert bleghan sine dó. 'Bennacht dée & anndée fort, a inghen', or Cú Culainn. Batar é a n-dée in t-aés cumhachta & a n-andée in t-aes trebaire, & bá slán in righan iarsin.*

149 Tuatha Dea (that is Donann) that is Gods the people of art and not-Gods the people of the populous; as Cú Chulain said because of the Taín Bó Cúailnge, when he was sorrowing and he had a great thirst after Lóch son of Mofeidbis had been killed. When Cú Chulainn was there in combat with Lóch, the Mórríghan daughter of Ernmas came towards him in a strange form out of the Fairymound to wound Cu Culainn during the combat. Cú Chulainn gave a cast at the Mórrighain in response breaking one of her eyes. She returned in the form of an old woman approaching Cu Culainn, and she was milking a cow with three teats in his presence. And it was for the sake of this therefore to get his help for her previous wounding by Cu Culainn, because any wounding of anyone by Cú Chulainn a portion of the act of healing must be treated by him himself. Cú Chulainn sought the milking on her because of the furious thirst. She gave the milking of a teat to him. 'May it be health not poison on me!' said Cú Chulainn. Health was then in one eye of the Queen. Because Cú Chulainn had broken her one eye before. He sought the milking of the other teat on her. She gave it to him. 'Not poison but may health be on her who grants this', said Cú Chulainn. He sought the third drink and she gave the milking of the teat to him. 'Blessing of Gods and not-gods on you, oh maiden', said Cú Culainn. These were their Gods the people of power and the not-Gods the people of husbandry, and after that the Queen was healthy.

150 *Dagda .i. dagh dé .i. día soinemhail ag na geintíbh é, ar do adhradháis Tuatha Dé Danann dó, ar bá día talmhan dóibh é ar mhét a chumachta.*

150 Dagda that is a good god that is an excellent god he was of the pagans; because the Tuatha De Danann adored/worshiped him, because he was a god of the world to them, because of the greatness of his power

151 *Eochaid Ollathair .i. uilliu é inna a athair. N[ó] ollathair .i. athair oll do Thuathaibh Dé Danann é.*

151 Eochaid Ollathair that is greater he than his father. Or ollathair that is ample father for the Tuatha Dé Danann.

152 *Ruadh Rofesa .i. is aigi robhoí óighi ind fessa g[e]inntlidhe, & is aigi bádar na tréidhe ildealbhaidhe.*

152 Ruadh Rofesa that is it was he who had the wholeness of heathen knowledge, and it is he who had the multi-formed accomplishments.

153 *Eochaid Bres .i. Eochaid cruthach, ar cach ní caem & cach ní cruthach atcíther ind Erinn is co Bres samhlaither .i. Breas mac Ealadhan meic Dhelbaith is fris atberar, & Eochaid ainm aile dó.*

153 Eochaid Bres that is Eochaid the beautiful, because every thing fair and every thing beautiful seen in Ireland is compared with Bres, that is Bres son of Elada son of Delbaeth is called thus, and Eochaid is the other name on him.

154 *Núadha Airgetlámh, cidh día tá? Ni ansa. A lamh dheas doben Sreng mac Senghainn de a comracc a cath Muighi Turedh Cunga, intan tangadar Túatha Dé Danann a n-Eirinn. Dochuiridar leaghaThúaithe Dé Danann lámh airgit co lánlúth cacha laimhe for Núadhait. Is aire sin tráth aderthi Núadha Airgétlámh friss iarsin.*

154 Núada Silver Hand, why thusly? Not difficult. His right arm was struck off by Sreng mac Senghainn in combat during the first battle of Muighi Turedh, when the Túatha Dé Danann came to Ireland. The physicians of the Túatha Dé Danann put a silver arm filled with the movement of every

arm on Núada. So that afterwards he then gets Núada Silver Hand on him.

155 Tuirenn Beggreann .i. grenn beg bhói fair .i. ba beg a ulcha. Dealbháeth ainm aile dó, & is do Thuirinn bá clánd in chlann remhraíti .i. clann Tuirinn .i. Brían & Eochaid & Iucharbha.

155 Tuirenn Beggreann that is a small beard was on him that is small was his beard. Delbáeth was the other name on him, and the children of Tuirinn where his children that is the family of Tuirinn that is Brían and Eochaid and Iucharba.

156 *Manannán mac Lir .i. Oirbsin a ainm. Oirbsiu proprium nomen eius Allaei nomen patris eius. .i. cendaighi amhra robí a n-Inis Manann .i. issé lúamhaire is dech robhí for muir a n-iarthar domain. Rofinnadh triana engnacht sic. leg. tria nemhghnacht, as in marg. sup. i. tría dheicsin ghné índ neime .i. ind aeoir, ind airet nóbhith in t-soininn nó in doininn, & intan conclaechlobadh cechtarde araile, & is aire sin rothoimnetar Bretnaigh & fir Erenn eissiumh gur' bhá dée in mhara é & Mac Lir aderthi fris .i. mac in mhara. Manannan dano do rádh ris a Manainn.*

156 Manannán mac Lir that is Oirbsin his name. Oirbsiu was his proper name Allaei the name of his father. That is a wonderful trader who was on the island of Man that is he was the best steersman on the sea in the west of the world. He knew through understanding, as it was actually written, through sky knowledge, that is through gazing at the appearance of the sky that is the air, the length of the world, the fine weather or stormy weather, and when the two elements would change each other, and the people of Britain and the men of Ireland called him the God of the sea and Mac Lir he was called that is son of the sea. Manannan moreover he was called for the Isle of Man.

157 *Dían Cecht .i. ainm suithe leigís Eirenn, dían na cumachta, nam cecht cumhachta dicitur, unde Néidhe mac Adhnai dixit: Cechtsam derca áthsgeanmaim ailcne .i. cumhachtaigsium ailcni .i. sceillec romhebaid don ailig condombí fri[a] súil-seom. Coni cáecsom .i. imrubhairt a chumhachta. Non est ut imperiti dicunt Cechtsum .i. cáechsum. Nó dian (.i. deus) caech (.i. sui). Ut est deus salúitis.*

157 Dían Cecht that is the name of the master physician of Ireland, swift the powers, for his learned powers it is said, whence Néidhe mac Adhnai said: An eye blinded by a splinter of rock purified that is using his power; splinter of rock, that is a small piece of stone, strikes to the other decreased against his eye. So that it is not 'blinds' but is 'strikes his powers'. That is not to say skilled powers but blinds. Or dian (that is a god) caech (that is learning). That is a god of healing.[85]

The St. Gall Incantations

A collection of healing charms from Cod. S. Galli No. 1395

(Against a Thorn)

Ni artu ní nim ni domnu ní muir arnóib bríathraib rolabrastar crist assa croich díuscart dím an delg delg díuscoilt crú ceiti méim méinni bé ái béim nand dodath scenn toscen todaig rogarg fiss goibnen aird goibnenn renaird goibnenn ceingeth ass:

Focertar in depaidse in im nadtét in uisce ocus fuslegar de imman delg immecuáirt ocus nitét fora n-airrinde nach fora n-álath ocus manibé an-delg and dotóeth in dala fiacail airthir a chin

Against a Thorn

"Nothing higher than heaven, nothing deeper than sea. On account of the powerful speech said by Christ on the cross, remove from me the thorn, a thorn pointedly-cleaves, wounds, destroys, in me there is an opening on account of striking, an unlucky appearance, frightening, a fire springs, very fierce Goibniu's knowledge, Goibniu's attention, Goibniu's powerful attention overcomes it":

Put the charm on the butter not into the water and smear around the thorn around its circumference and not on the cut nor on the affliction, and if there is no thorn in it will fall out the second spike[86] from the front of his head.

(Against urinary disease)

Ár gálár fúail;

Dumesursca diangalar fúailse dunesairc éu ét dunescarat eúin énlaithi admai ibdach;

Focertar inso dogrés imaigin hitabair thúal :

prechnytosan (i.e. praedicent) omnibus nationibus FINIT:

Against urinary disease

"I am saved from sudden illness of urine, I am saved from salmon envy, I am saved from birds, skillful flocks, spell-workers."

Display this always where you habitually go to pour out.

publish to all nations, the end

(Against headache)

Caput christi oculus isaiæ frons nassium nóe labia lingua salomonis collum temathei mens beniamín pectus pauli iunctus iohannis fides abrache sanctus sanctus sanctus dominus deus sabaoth

Canir anisiu cach dia im du chenn ar chenn galar iarna gabáil dobir da sale it bais ocus dabir imdu da are ocus fort chulatha ocus cani du pater fothrí lase 7 dobir cros ditsailiu forochtar do chinn ocus dogní atóirandsa dano U fort chiunn

Against headache

"Head of Christ, eye of Isaiah, bridge of the nose of Noah, lips and tongue of Solomon, in mind Benjamin, breast-joined John Paul's faith abrache Holy, holy, holy is the Lord God of hosts",

This is sung each day around your head against illnesses of the head. After take spring water putting it through your palms and put it around your two temples and on the back of your neck, and sing your Our Father three times by it, and put a cross for that reason of spring water on the top of your head, and then make this therefore, U, on your head.

(Against various ailments)

"Tessurc marb bíu. Ar díring, ar goth-sring, ar att díchinn, ar fuilib híairn, ar ul loscas tene, ar ub hithes cú. Rop achuh rú ,crinas teoracnoe, crete teoraféthe fichte, benim a galar ar fiuch fuili guil Fuil nirub att rée rop slán frosaté admuinur in slánicid foracab Diancecht lia muntir corop slán ani forsate"

focertar inso dogrés itbois láin di uisciu ocindlut ocus dabir itbéulu ocus imbir indamér atanessam dolutain itbélaib cechtar ái áleth

Against various ailments

"I save the dead-alive. Against belching, against javelin-cord, against unkind swelling, against iron wounds, against an edge fire burned, against a point a dog bites. Let him be sharply-red, three nuts withering, believe that three sinews are woven. I strike his illness, I overcome wounds lamenting of blood. Let it not be an endless swelling. Let him be healthy, pouring on I invoke the salve left by Dian Cecht with his family that what it is poured on be whole."

Set this always in your palm full of water while washing, and thou put it in your mouth, and use the two fingers that are next the little-finger in your mouth, each of them separate.

The Klostrneuburg Incantation

A magical chant for protection. The Irish text is taken from Irish from E., Hermann. 1871

---

1. *Cris finnáin dumimdegail imum imacuáirt.*
nar amtairthea innsét timcellas intuáith

Protection of Finnan's belt around me encircling
I shall not be seized on the road going around the country

2. *Raucthi láin induleán mubrond.*
lurech dé dumimdegail otamind gombond.

Completely encirlces my defenseless belly
God's corslet to me protection around me from head to foot

3. *Cris fimieain muchris argalar arches*
aruptaib banmbeth afraech adamles.

Belt of my poisonous birds, my belt for sickness, for debility
From slaying of fair life and from fury, from loss

4. *Cris eoin muchris ralég súidi nglan.*
daid ferga fer soid upta mban.

A bird belt, my belt exactly placed it is
For wrathful men, defeats magic of women

5. *Cris nathrach muchris nathair imátá*
náramgonat fir naramillet mná.

Serpent belt, my belt of snakes it is around me
It wounds men, it destroys women.

6. *durennaib romóra fomóir imátá*
Fortitude of the great Fomorians is around me

7. *Fobrut muridam fosarabi inrí.*
fotrochlanib fochochlan mubí.

Beneath an abundant cloak, for me an excellent surety fit for a king
Released beneath my little hood my face

8. *Mucholmoc ramcharastar arfégad arfis.*
isairai ramcharastar uair istend mochris.

My Colmoc has love for me, because of seeing it, knowing it
It is instigating this loving because of the strength of my belt

Holidays

Several excerpts focused on Lunasa, Imbolc, and Bealtaine. Further material on the holidays can be found in chapter 6.

"Co brón trogein .i. lugnusad .i. taide fogamuir .i. is and dobroine trogain .i. talom fo toirtip. Trogan didiu ainm do talum."
Meyer, K., (1910). Tochmarc Emire la Coinculaind, page 246

"Until Brón Trogain, that is, Lunasa, that is the beginning of autumn, that is, then the earth is sorrowing, that is, earth under fruit. Trogan is another name for earth."

Belltaine .i. bil tene .i. tene ṡoinmech .i. dáthene dognítis druidhe tria thaircedlu ...móraib combertis na cethrai arthedmannaib cacha bliadna cusnaténdtibsin (MARG-L eictis na cethra etarru)
Sanas Cormaic B102, (n.d.)

Bealtaine, meaning lucky fire or fire of abundance, a festival with two fires made by Druidic incantations...made for the young herds to receive blessing every year against illnesses [note - the herds need to be driven between the fires]

Co ndénta a cluiche cacha bliadna ic Lugnasad .i. Coícthiges ria lugnasad & coicthiges iar lugnasad. Lugnasad .i. noasad Loga meic Eithnend ainm in chluiche.
Macalister, R., (1940). Lebor Gabala Erenn

With a festival every year at Lúnasa, that is 15 days before Lúnasa and 15 days after Lúnasa. Lúnasa, that is a death commemoration Lugh son of Eithne named the festival.

iar n-imbulc, ba garb a ngeilt
after Imbolc, rough was their herding
From *the Metrical Dindshenchas*

On Various Gods

Various excerpts that mention different deities.

Maiche .i. bodb; ł isi in tres morrigan .i. maiche 7 bodb 7 morrigan, unde mesrad maiche .i. cenna daoine iarna nairlech, ut dixit dub ruis. Garbæ adbae innon fil. i lomrad fir maiche mes, i nagat laich liu i lles, i lluaiget mna trogain tres.
Irsan, Dublin, Trinity College, MS 1337 (H.3.18), pp. 79c–83b

Macha, that is a crow, one of the three Morrigans, that is Macha and Badb and Morrigan. Whence the harvest of Macha, that is men's heads after the slaughter, having said that, dark red [or 'who said that, Dub Ruis']. Rough dwellings are over there. Where men sheer off Macha's crop, where warriors drive a multitude into pens, where the raven women cause battles.

Machæ .i. badb. nó así an tres morrígan, unde mesrad Machæ i. cendæ doine iarna n-airlech
O'Mulconry's Glossary, (n.d.)

Macha, that is Badb or one of the three Morrigans, whence Macha's harvest that is people's heads after the slaughter.

Macha i. badhb, no feannóg. mol macha i. cruinniughadh badhb, no feannóg
O'Clery's Glossary, (n.d.)

Macha, that is a crow or hooded crow, the heap[87] of Macha that is the collection[88] of crows or hooded crows.
Fuil os chind ag eigmigh
Caillech lom, luath ag leimnig
Os eannaib a narm sa sciath

Is i in Morrigu mongliath
Cath Magh Rath

Bloody over his head, fighting, crying out
A naked hag, swiftly leaping
Over the edges of their armor and shields
She is the grey-haired Morrigu

"Badb is Macha mét indbáis,
Morrigan fotla felbáis,
Indlema ind ága ernbais,
Ingena ana Ernmais."
Book of Leinster, folio 5

Badb and Macha, important treasure,
Morrigan, wealth of spells,
Surrounding death by sword's edge
Rich daughters of Ernmas"

H-i Ross Bodbo i. na Morrighno, ar iss ed a ross-side Crich Roiss ocus iss i an bodb catha h-i ocus is fria id-beurur bee Neid i. bandee in catæ, uair is inann be Neid ocus dia cathæ.
Meyer, K., (1910). Tochmarc Emire

In the Wood of Badb, that is of the Morrigu, therefore her proven-wood the land of Ross, and she is the Battle-Crow and is also called the woman of Neit, that is Goddess of Battle, because Neit is also a God of Battle.

Ré secht mbliadan Nuadat narsheng
Osin chuanairt chéibfind
Flathius ind fir chichmair chuilfind
Ria tiachtain in Hérind
I Maig Thuiredh, truim co trucha,

I torchair cuing in chatha,
Do cosnamaid bán in betha -
Ro lead a lám flatha.
Macalister, R., (1940). Lebor Gabala Erenn

A space of seven years noble, graceful Nuada
Over a fair-haired warrior-pack
Ruled the greatly keen, fair-tressed man
Before going to Ireland
In Maige Tuired, heavy with doom,
By chance burden in the battle
From the bright defender of life -
Hacked off was his arm of sovereignty.

Brigit .i. banfile ingen in Dagdai. is eiside Brigit baneceas (ł be neicsi) .i. Brigit bandee noadradís filid. arba romor 7 baroán afri thgnam. is airesin ideo eam (deam) uocant poetarum hoc nomine cuius sorores erant Brigit be legis Brigit bé goibnechta .i. bandé .i. tri hingena in Dagdai insin. de quarum nominibus pene omnes Hibernenses dea Brigit uocabatur. Brigit din .i. breoaigit l breoṡaigit.

Sanas Cormaic B 129

Literal translation - Brigit, that is a poet daughter of the Dagda. It is this Brigit woman of poetic art (woman of the poetic skill) that is Brigit Goddess worshiped by poets. Great benefit and great service is hers. It is therefore she is called a Goddess by poets; her sisters were Brigit the woman of healing, Brigit the woman of smithcraft, that is a Goddess, that is they are three daughters of the Dagda. Of which names almost all Irish goddesses are called Brigit. Brigit, then that is breoaigit or breoshaigit fiery arrow.

Assorted

Sonus lomma is lenna lir,
buáid comairle in cech caingin,
búaid comperta, clú co mbail,
búaid creiche adiu, buáid slúagaid.
Trí lán ma chluic d'usci úar
do chur esti a n-agaid slúag,
innreth t'innse tairis sin
Betha Colmáin maic Lúacháin

Luck of milk and plentiful beer,
Victory of counsel in every matter,
Victory of judgments, fame with good luck,
Victory raiding henceforth, victory of hosts
three full good bells of cold water
Your horse-champions towards the faces of the host
Injury to those there forth

Untitled
Grainne to Fionn
ut dixit Gránni ingen Cormaic fri Find.
'Fil duine
rismad buide lemm díuderc,
ara tribrinn, la dia tribrend, in m-bith ule, la m-buide,
la h-uile h-uile, cid díupert.'
marginalia Amra Columb Chille

Spoken by Grainne daughter of Cormac to Fionn:
"There is a person
On whom I would gladly look,
Who I would give, would give the entire world, the world,
all of it, even if it is a fraud."

Trí coiri bíte in cach dúini: coire érma, coire goriath, coire áiged
Triads of Ireland

Three cauldrons are in every person: a cauldron of motion, a cauldron of warming,[89] a cauldron of honor

Fírinde inár croidhedhaibh ocus nertt inár lámhaibh, ocus comall inár tengthaibh - Acallam na Senórach

Truth in our hearts, and strength in our arms, and fulfillment of duty in our tongues

Ní dlig ferann fer cen treoir,
ní dlig degairm fer cen gliaid,
ní dlig cerchaill cenn co mbeoil,
ní dlig feoil fer cen scíain.
marginalia Harleian 5280

Not deserving of land is a man without action
Not deserving of armoring is a man without battle skill
Not deserving of a pillow is a greasy head
Not deserving of meat is a man without a knife

Adfenar fó fiu.
Adfenar olcc anmoínib.
Adfenar maith moínib.
Cethairshlicht Athgabálae

Good is repaid by worthiness
Bad is repaid by un-treasures
Excellence is repaid by treasures

A Blessing:
"Corbat cara sluaig,
Corbat roga ríg,
Corbat cruithnecht chaem,
Corbat craebh co fín."
A Maccáin Na Cí

May you be a crowd's friend
May you be a king's selection
May you be valuable wheat
May you be a branch with wine

Various Curses:
"Ferr gach maoin mainbthigh miofhocal már marta"
Bretha Nemed Dédenach

Better than every wealth of treasure, a great slaughterous curse

"Fognad dúib ág is ernbas"
The Metrical Dindshenchas

May you all be served dark battle and iron-death[90]
"Bé Néit fort"
Sanas Cormaic, #168

Goddess of Battle on you

"Bás fort béolu"
Fingal Rónáin

Death on your mouth[91]
An Idiomatic Saying:
"Íbait fíaich lúgbairt lacht!"
The Táin Bó Cúailgne; Leabhar Buidhe Lecain

Literally - "Ravens will drink milk of a garden"
Figuratively - "Ravens will drink blood of a battlefield"

Chapter 6

Poetry

I'm wrapping up this book with an assortment of poetic pieces that cover everything from Vikings to magical prayers to the famous '*Pangur Bán*'. I hope readers enjoy the range of options here.

Is Acher in Gáith Innocht

> A short poem found in the marginalia of a book, expressing the scribe's feelings at the time. A beautiful and evocative piece and one of my personal favourites. Irish from Meyer (1911)

Is acher in gaíth innocht,
fu-fúasna fairgge findfolt:
ní ágor réimm mora minn
dond láechraid lainn ó Lothlainn

Fierce is the wind tonight
Agitating the ocean's white hair;
I do not fear advancing across the sea
Eager dark warriors of Norway

Cétemain, Cain Cucht

The following is a poem said to have been spoken by Finn Mac Cumal in praise of May. The Irish text is from Meyer (1903)

Cétemain, cain cucht
Mayday, Beautifully Formed

1 Cétemain, cain cucht,
rée rosaír rann;
canait luin laíd láin
día laí (grían) gaí n-gann.

1 Mayday, beautifully formed,
time moves forward in its division;
the blackbird clearly sings his songs
praise of day's (sun's) scarce spear

2 Gairid cuí chrúaid den;
is fo-chen sam saír:
suidid síne serb
i m-bi cerb caill chraíb.

2 The rough-colored cuckoo calls;
to welcome summer's arrival:
settled is a bitter age
in entering a silver forest of trees.

3 Cerbaid sam súaill sruth;
saigid graig lúath linn;
lethaid fota fraích;
for-beir folt fann finn.

3 Summer cuts short a trifling river;
seeking out swift water horses;
extending long hair;
growing hair soft and shining.

4 Fúapair sceith scell scíach;
im-reith réid rían rith;
cuirithir sál súan;
tuigithir bláth bith.

4 Dashing attacks on a warrior's shield;
the sea's path rotates easily;
causing the sea's magical sleep;
flowers covering the world.

5 Berait beich (bec nert)
bert bonn bochtai bláith;
berid slabrai slíab:
feraid saidbir sáith.

5 Bees carry (little strength)
a burden of wild angelica, gathering flowers;
cattle go up the mountains:
supplying a sufficiency of wealth.

6 Seinnid caille céol;
con-greinn séol síd slán;
síatair denn do dinn,
dé do loch linn lán.

6 The harp plays music;
music gathering in complete peace;
color settled on every height,
haze from the lake full of waters.

7 Labraid tragna trén;
canaid ess n-ard n-úag
fáilti do (thoinn) té;
táinic lúachra lúad.

7 The corncrake speaks strongly;
a young, high waterfall sings
welcome to the warm (wave);
discussion of rushes has come.

8 Lengait fainnle fúas;
(im-said) crúas cíuil (cróich)
for-beir mes máeth méth;
(innisid loth loíth).

8 The swallow freely leaps;
(circling) a gentle song (the hill)
crops growing soft and rich;
(the stammering marsh announces).

9 (Leig lath fath feig);
(fert) ar-cain cuí chrúaid;
cuirithir brecc bedc;
is balc (gedc) láith lúaith.

9 (The warrior stone's covering is luminous);
a (grave-mound) cuckoo sings sternly;
leaps away the speckled [fish];
powerful are the (may-fly) swift warriors.

10 Losaid foirbríg fer;
óg a m-búaid m-breg m-bras;
caín cach caille clár;
caín cach mag már mas.

10 Men's vigor grows;
youths of victory, fitness, boastfulness;
beautiful every forest plain;
beautiful every great plain's foundation.

11 Melldach rée rann;
(ro fáith) gaíth garb gam;
gel ros; toirthech (tonn);
(oll) síd; subach sam.

11 Delightful quarter of time;
(gone are) rough winter winds;
bright woods; fruitful (wave);
(great) peace; cheerful summer.

12 Suidigthir íall én
(i n-íath) i m-bí ben;
búirithir gort glas
i m-bí bras glas gel.

12 A flock of birds settles
(in a territory) in abundance;
noise in green fields
in loud living bright green.

13 Greit mer, imrim ech;
im-sernar sreth slúaig;
rosáer rath geilestar:
ór eilestar úaid.

13 A wild hero, riding horses;
the ordered host is arrayed around;
crafted a fort's cattle pond:
the water-source gold underneath.

14 *Ecal aird fer fann;*
fedil fochain ucht;
uiss ima-cain
'Cetemain, cain cucht'.

14 A timid weak person's attention;
enduring call in the air;
larks singing around
'Maytime, beautifully formed'.

Folamh anocht Dún Chearmna
Dun Cearmna is empty tonight

Folamh anocht Dún Chearmna
do Ráith Teamhra is cúis bhaoghail;
mad uaigneasa an dúin dreachglain –
beart do bheartaibh an tsaoghail.

Dun Cearmna is empty tonight
From the Fort of Tara is a dangerous cause;
Surrounded by desolation the bright-fronted fort
An exploit of the arrow your task[92]

Ríoghradh fhial an dúin duasbhuig
ar nach bíodh uamhain foghla,
dá n-éis is truagh mar táimsi,
'sgan ann acht áite folmha.

The generous fort of noble kings
Who had no fear of attack
It is after wretched as a ghost
Without him there it is but a desolate place

Gearr go rabhad 'na n-uathadh,
Ráth Chruachan is Ráth Teamhra
gá beag dóibh so do robhadh? –
folamh anocht Dún Chearmna.

A small time of warning for the few,
Fort of Cruachan and Fort of Tara
Is another small warning needed for you?
Dun Cearmna is empty tonight

Fothart for trebaib Con Corbb
The Fothart among the Household of Concorb

The Irish was transcribed from MS Rawlinson B 502

Fothart for trebaib Con Corbb
ri Temair cid rodas terb
Eochu Fuath Airt erctha gluind
fri Art mac Cuind gabthais fergg.

The Fothart among the household of Concorb
It was the king of Tara who separated them
Eochu Fuath Airt, an evil deed,
Against Art son of Conn conceived [in] anger.

Dia roinned a dám i nnóe
ocon mnaí co fad in rí
na fairsed Lagniu iar lín fer
mac ríg Breg di Boinne brí.

When the warriors went in ships
without women around the king
the firm Leinsterman afterwards a full complement of men
Son of royal Breg from the hill of Boinne.

Brigit ba dia chlaind iar céin
sluindfet mar gréin glan a níab
mac huí Echdach ba fíu ríg
ba díb Fintan fethlach fial

Brigit was with the household long afterwards
Named like the healing sun's vigour

Son descended of Echdach he is intended [as] a king
He is of Fintan's honourable likeness

Brigit & Fintan find
conacnat frim siu & tall;
di omnai óir as mo thur
úaim dóib eter bun is barr.

Brigit and fair Fintan
Help to me here and there;
Two golden oaks from my cultivation
A pool to drink between beginning and end.

Mo siur mo brathair beó
anad a breó fri cech ró
ro thríal mo chiall cairdes friu
sech ba fial ba fíu ba fó.

My sister, my brother in life
Its life withstands against every trial
Travelled my wise friendship forward
That is it was honourable, it was worthy, it was good.

Ced ros ndechaid assa thír
Eochuid Breg dom brecdais géil;
mac Feidlimthi Rectaid rúaid
do chúain Túathail Techtmair thréin.

Why departed out of his country,
Powerful Echu, for my bright [?];
the son of Fedelmid Rechtaid
of the race of mighty Tuathal Techtmar.

Hécin ris ndechaid immach
Echuid ria cath clú ro chleth.
leis dobert fri selba sreth
cleth cáirthind i Temra tech.

It was by force [he] went abroad
Echu departing before a battle under secrecy,
by him had been brought in his own array
a spear of rowan into the house of Tara.

Dobreth cend fir forsin cleith
ar scáth in scéith ba bil braith;
demin leis ba hed ind sein
mescfad in fleid immon flaith.

The head of a man had been put on the spear
behind the shield rim, it was treachery;
he knew well that that was what would
disrupt the feast for the ruler.

Iar sain atbert ris in druí
Mac Da Chúr nad chanad gaí
dobreth cleth chairthind co crú
tre thnú issin tech i taí.

Then the druid said to him
Da Chúr's son who never spoke false
'A rowan spear with gore was brought
enviously into the house in stealth.'

Frisin druid adféded cert
atbert oenrí Herend Art;
cia don tslúag ro choirp in tech?
ca airm i tá in chleth? cluinem lat.

To the druid who was revealing truth
Art, the high-king of Ireland, said;
'Who of the host brought the corpse in the house?
Where is the spear? Let us hear it from you.'

Lassais leis in chleth co crú.
ra anacht in tech nir on dó.
in druí ciarbo demin lais a chlí
adsuí tenid co fí fó.

Flared up then the spear with gore.
the house was saved, no disgrace to him,
The druid therefore with his authority
kindles a fire with knowing venom.

Eochaid Fuath Airt & Cond
Fiacha Suidge síd glond ngrind.
nídam eligthe dia sluind
roptar meic Feidlimthi find.

'Eochu Fuath Airt and Conn
Descendants of Fiacha Suidge
I am accusing with this declaration
They are the sons of fair Feidlimthi'

Brathir duilge dún fria fis.
cland Fiachach Suidge serb gus.
triar leoman lotar fodes.
Oengus is Eogan is Rus.

Harsh considerations towards them from the fort
Family of Fiacha Suidge's bitter deed
Three lions had gone outwards
Oengus and Eogan and Rus

Diaro choill Oengus elgna in gein.
rosc ríg Temra assa thuil;
doringni galgait iar sein
Cellach mac Cormaic do guin

A violation Oengus had caused in malice the injury
Chanted the king of Tara out of his will:
'He made a violation then there
Cellach son of Cormac to slay

Ro carta a Bregaib a Brí
a Slemain a Sléib Trí nDé
trebsat Femen co n-ír
co ndernsat tir ndiles de.

Drive away from Brega from Bri
From Slemain from Sléib Trí nDé
Inhabiting Femen with anger
They have forfeited their own land.'

Na Dési Muman mór chath
úan a mbunad buidnib cloth;
Oengus Eogan acher bruth
Rus is Fothud cona foth.

The Desi of Munster, great troops,
From their family's famous war-band
Oengus, Eogan, sharp valour,
Rus and Fothud without a claim

Colum Cille ba gein glan
brathair dil dam acht mo chel
Colum co crábud co ngrís
dom snádud iar n-aís for nem.

Colum Cille was born pure
Beloved brother to me until my death
Colum with devotion and ardour
To me protection then under heaven

Brigit form deis tall sund síu.
Colum do chlíu ni geis dó
do síl Chrimthaind Níad Náir
ríg tairmchell firu Fail fó.

Brigit on land hereafter here
Colum to territories without prohibitions
Seed of Crimthann Nia Nair
King encircling Ireland's men around

Galenga Delmna ní adiú.
Ciannacht im Chenna ní gó.
co cath Crinna cend fri ard
dia tarbart Tadc firu fó. F.

Galeng Delbnae not from this place
Ciannacht in Cenna without falsehood
With pure Crinna chief to the height
When viewing Tadg's men under Fothart

Quatrains on Festivals

A poem about the four fire festivals, describing the qualities of each celebration and time of year in turn. Irish text was transcribed from Bodleian Library MS. Rawl. B. 502

Atberim frib, lith saine,
ada buada belltaine:
coirm, mecoin, suabais serig,
ocus urgruth do tenid.

I tell to you, an excellent festival,
suitably pre-eminent is Bealtaine:
ale-feasts, edible roots, gentle bitters,
and new curds for a fire.

Lugnassad, luaid a hada
cecha bliadna ceinmara,
fromad cech toraid co m-blaid,
biad lusraid la Lugnasaid.

Lúnasa, suitably it moves
each year along,
tasting every fruit of harvesting,
food herbs with Lúnasa.

Carna, cuirm, cnoimes, cadla,
it e ada na samna,
tendal ar cnuc co n-grinde,
blathach, brechtan urimme.

Meat, beer, nuts, tripe,
they are suitable food for Samhain,
bonfire on a hill with a company,
buttermilk, a roll of new butter.

Fromad cach bíd iar n-urd,
issed dlegair i n-Imbulc,
díunnach laime is coissi is cinn,
is amlaid sin atberim.

Tasting each food for freshness,
this is the principle at Imbolc,
cleansing hands and feet and head,
Thus I say to you.

Lugh's Arrival at Teamhair

This is an excerpt from a 14th century poem; this portion is telling about Lugh's arrival at Tara during the larger story of the Cath Maige Tuired. The Irish text is taken from *Mór ar bhfearg riot, ri Saxan*

Tabhás do Lugh, leannán Teamhra
thoir i nEamhain,
dá ránaig sé ar súr gach domhain
Múr Té, Teamhair.

Revealed to Lugh, lover of Teamhra
in the east in Eamhain,[93]
so he went to search the whole earth for
Té's Ramparts, Teamhair [Tara].

Dúnta an chathair ar chionn Logha,
laoch ro thoghsom;
téid gusan múr sleamhain slioschorr
beanaidh boschrann.

Closed was the city against Lugh's arrival,
the choicest of warriors;
touched with force the sharp-sided, smooth ramparts
struck the door-wood.

Ar an doirseóir ris an deaghlaoch,
fá doirbh ruaigfhearg:
cáit as a dtig an fear áith ógard
bláith geal gruaiddearg.

The King's doorman said to the great warrior,
whose anger was swift:
"From where comes the man, keen, young,
bright flower, red cheeked."

Ris an doirseóir
a dubhairt Lugh nár loc iomghuin:
file meise a hEamhain Abhlaigh
ealaigh iobhraigh.

To the King's Doorman
said Lugh who never hesitated in reciprocal wounding:
"I am myself a poet of Eamhain Abhlach
of swans and yews."

"Nocha dligi", ar doirseóir Teamhra,
"tocht diar ndaighthigh;
atá fear ri"

"Not merited", said Teamhair's doorman,
"Coming from conflict;
There is a kingly man"

Pangur Bán

Pangur Bán is one of the better-known Old Irish poems, a work from around the 9th century which details the exploits -academic and hunting - of a scholar and his cat. The following Old Irish is from Stokes *Thesaurus Paleohibernicus,* from 1903.

Messe ocus Pangur bán,
cechtar nathar fria saindán;
bíth a menma-sam fri seilgg,
mu menma céin im saincheirdd

Myself and Fair Pangur
both of us with our tasks;
for his mind is on hunting,
my mind on each separate art

Caraim-se fós, ferr cach clú,
oc mu lebrán léir ingnu;
ní foirmtech frimm Pangur bán,
caraid cesin a maccdán.

I love the quiet, better than fame,
and my book zealously I study
no envy against me has Fair Pangur
he loves his own youthful skill

Ó ru-biam scél cén scis
innar tegdias ar n-oéndis,
táithiunn dichríchide clius
ní fris 'tarddam ar n-áthius.

Where we are adventuring without rest
here in our house, the single pair
we have unlimited feats
of acuteness to apply against something

Gnáth-huaraib ar greassaib gal
glenaid luch ina lín-sam;
os me, du-fuit im lín chéin
dliged ndoraid cu n-dronchéill.

Usually his furious attack
catches a mouse up in his net:
my eye, my own net, reaches
a difficult concept that is well hidden

Fúachaid-sem fri freaga fál
a rosc a nglése comlán;
fúachimm chéin fri fégi fis
mu rosc réil, cesu imdis.

He sharpens his skill against these
his eye is the perfect tool for this
I direct my clear eye, though very weak
towards sharpening knowledge

Fáelid-sem cu n-déne dul,
hi nglen luch ina gérchrub;
hi-tucu cheist n-doraid n-dil,
os mé chene am fáelid.

He rejoices with his swift snaring
Cleaving a mouse in his sharp claws
I grasp a question, difficult, dear,
and my mind in that time is happy

Cia beimini amin nach ré
ní derban cách a chéle;
mait le cechtar nár a dán
subaigthiud a óenurán.

Even if we work thus every time
neither hinders the other one;
good we each are at our skill
rejoicing when alone

Hé fesin as choimsid dáu
in muid du-n-gní cach óenláu;
do thabairt doraid du glé
for mumud céin am messe.

He himself is capable of the purpose
at the work he does every single day;
to bring a dark thing to light
at my own work, am I

Cétnad nAíse

A poem which is also in its way a prayer and magical chant for protection and for long life. The poem itself is difficult to parse but Tonsing suggests in his analysis of it that it is primarily a pagan piece with very little clear Christina influence. Irish text was found unattributed at https://www.maryjones.us/ctexts/cetnad.html

---

Ad-muiniur secht n-ingena trethan
dolbtae snáithi macc n-áesmar.
Tri bás flaimm ro-ucaiter,
tri áes dom do-rataiter,

I invoke the seven daughters of the stormy sea
shaping life's thread from boyhood to age
Three deaths be taken from me
Three ages be given to me

secht tonna tocaid dom do-ra-dáilter!
Ním chollet messe fom chúairt
i llúrig lasréin cen léiniud!
Ní nassar mo chlú ar chel!

Seven waves of good fortune dispense to me!
No harm to me on my circuit
in flashing corslet without hindering!
Not light is my reputation before heaven!

dom-í-áes;
nim thi bás comba sen!
Ad-muiniur m'Argetnia
nád bá nád bebe;

To me these ages
May I not die until old age
I invoke my Silver warrior
who did not die and will not die

amser dom do-r-indnastar
findruini febe!
Ro orthar mo richt,
ro saerthar mo recht,

Deliver to me time
of excellent electrum!
Chanting my form,
Ennobling my authority,

ro mórthar mo nert,
nip ellam mo lecht,
nim thí bás for fecht,
ro firthar mo thecht!

Magnified my strength,
Not readied my grave,
May I not die on a journey,
My death fulfilled!

Ním ragba nathair díchonn,
ná dorb dúrglass,
ná doel díchuinn!

May a foolish serpent not overtake me,
Nor a hard-green worm,
Nor a senseless beetle!

Ním millither téol,
ná cuire ban,
ná cuire buiden!

May no theft destroy me
Nor host of women
Nor warrior troop!

Dom-i urchar n-aimsire
ó Rig inna n-uile!
Ad-muiniur Senach sechtaimserach
con-altatar mná side
far bruinnib bdais.

To me extensions of time
From the King of everything!
I invoke Senach of seven-durations
Who was reared by Fairy women
on their breasts.

Ní báitter mo shechtchaindel!
Am dun díthagail,
am all anscuichthe,
am ha lógmar,
am sen sechtmainech.

May my seven lights not be submerged!
I am an indestructable fort,
I am an immovable foundation,
I am that treasure
I am seven-times-valuable compensation

Roba chétach
cétbliadnach,
cach cét diib ar úair.
Cota-gaur cucum mo lessa;

May I be possessing a hundred
hundred years
Every hundred from each hour.
I sue towards me my advantage

ro bé rath in Spiurta Noíb formsa.
Domini est salus.
Christis est salus.
Super populum tuum, Domine, benedictio tua.

May the grace of the Holy Spirit be on me
The Lord is salvation
Christ is salvation
On your people, Lord, your blessing

Scél Lemm Dúib

Dated to the 8th or 9th century this short piece is a very evocative description of the end of summer and beginning of winter. Irish text from Meyer (1903)

Ut dixit Find hu Baiscne:
Scél lemm dúib:
Dordaid dam,
Snigid gaim,
Ro-fáith sam;
Gáeth ard úar,
Ísel grían,
Gair a rith,
Ruirthech rían;
Ro-rúad rath
Ro-cleth cruth,
Ro-gab gnáth
Guigrann guth;
Ro-gab úacht
Etti én
Aigre re
É mo scél.
9th century Irish

As Fionn descendant of Baiscne said:
I have news for you:
The stag bells,
Winter snows,
Summer has gone;
Wind high and cold,
The sun low,
Short its course

The sea running high;
Deep red the bracken
Its shape lost,
The wild goose has
Raised its accustomed cry;
Cold has seized
The birds' wings
Season of ice
This is my news.

Fáed Fíada - aka the Deer's Cry

The oldest part of Saint Patrick's Lorica this section is thought to date back, possibly, into the pagan period and to reference the magical ability to pass invisibly which was a skill of the Aos Sidhe and Tuatha De Danann.

Atomriug indiu
niurt nime,
soilsi gréne,
étrochtai éscai,
áni thened,
déni lóchet,
luaithi gaíthe,
fudomnai mara,
tairismigi thalman,
cobsaidi ailech.

I bind today
strength of sky
light of sun
radiance of moon
brightness of flame
swiftness of light
speed of wind
depth of ocean
steadfastness of earth
firmness of rock.

Endnotes

1. Sidhe is a complex word which might best be understood as 'Otherworldly mounds/hills' although it is often given as fairy hills. In modern language it is also sometimes used for the beings who inhabit those hills, the Aos Sidhe [people of the Otherworldly hills].
2. This is a bit awkward to render in English. Literally it's "Spent is your legitimate guest to you then".
3. Dagda – good god.
   Ruad Rofhessa - Red of great knowledge.
   Eochaid Ollathair – horseman great-father, with oll – "great" meaning large or immense rather than exceptionally good.
4. "Minbeoil" means either small mouth or gentle mouth, depending on whether there is a fada over the i in min or not. I personally favor mín, gentle, docile, courteous, although self-restrained may be a bit odd as an epithet for a deity who slept with the high king's wife.
   I find it interesting if it is minbeoil (small mouthed) that begbeoil, also meaning small mouthed, is one of the Morrigan's given names in the Tain Bo Regamna.
5. In the original the three items alliterate "lene, lorg, ocus lomann" the first can be understood as a tunic or shirt, the second as a staff or stick, so going with shirt and staff we can keep a bit of the alliteration, but lomann is usually understood as cloak, however there are references in the Metrical Dindshenchas where it is translated as "shield", and I have gone with this translation as it then preserves the alliteration that the original Old Irish possessed.
6. Beothach means living, a living creature.
7. More colloquially "you are right".
8. sidhe, later sí, ie fairy hills or fairies.

9. fo chen, seems to be an idiomatic expression, similar to mo chen, indicating a nod or bow, probably a welcome or greeting.
10. Bruig Macc ind Oicc, holding of the Young Son, is an older name of Brugh na Bóinn or Newgrange.
11. Lake of the Dragon Mouth.
12. Bruig Maicc ind Oicc, that is Newgrange.
13. Also, in this line caem could be read as beautiful rather than fitting/suitable.
14. Locha Dá Líg probably means lake of two glories.
15. In fairness this could also read "seek birds", but attack seemed to better fit the overall tone of the poem.
16. Thethbí - may be interpreted as "killing threshold".
17. The name "Da Airbe Bíat" may mean "two numerous armies" or "two yew fences".
18. Be Find, literally "White woman" but also meaning "bright woman" or "fair woman".
19. Oenuch Bodbgnai - Harvest fair of the beautiful crow.
20. Rucht has various meanings, including a pig, a noise or cry, or madness.
21. Ingen – nail, hoof, claw, talon, etc.
22. Eitte – wing or feather.
23. A whale.
24. Possibly a form of blad, fame or renown.
25. Rind, the point of a weapon.
26. From faebar a sharp-edged weapon.
27. A shadow or spectre, but can also mean protection; given its paired with sciath I would tend to read it as protection or shielding.
28. A shield.
29. White-horned of Ai.
30. Brown of Cooley.
31. This may be better relay.ed in English as "You must think I'm an idiot to tell me this" ie he thinks they are intentionally playing with him.

32. literally cleittíne a small dart or javelin which was one of Cu Chulain's particular weapons.
33. The majority of the Irish material here is from the Yellow Book of Lecan version, however the Morrigan's satire poem is the von Egerton version, both found in Windisch's Irische Texte mit Ubersetzugen and Worterbuchen.
34. This line is a point of contention in many translations, because the word ditin is uncertain. It can be read as a form of díden, to bring about or lead to, or it can be read as a form of dídiu, to shelter, protect, or guard. In other translations you may see this line presented as "I am guarding your death" which can be, and often is, interpreted in a protective manner. I however favour the díden view, as does the eDIL, and am giving it here as 'bringing about your death' which both fits the feelings of the current text and the wider actions of the Morrigan in relation to Cu Chulainn.
35. For those who are interested in the use of color in Irish material it's given here as glas, or green, but green which can be anything from a light green or blue to a blue grey.
36. Because Cu Chulainn is the son of the Tuatha De Danann Lugh any wound he inflicts cannot be healed except if he allows it to be.
37. See previous footnote for discussion of use of "green" to mean blue-grey.
38. In Old Irish "fír fer" literally "men's truth". This concept is the bases of honorable combat in Irish warfare and hinges on the idea of one-on-one fighting of equal opponents.
39. Cor is a word for a bird that can be a heron, crane or occasionally stork.
40. Strong.
41. A ferry.
42. Illness.
43. Either a sign or mark or else spit.
44. Uncertain but possible a wand or goad.

45. Quarrel or fight.
46. Grouse or warrior.
47. Son of Grece (see previous note).
48. Ger and gér both mean sharp or keen.
49. Dír – proper, suitable, fitting.
50. Salach means dirty, so this would be read as Ecet the dirty.
51. Calf.
52. Greth – a nutshell.
53. A cumal was a measure of value usually equated to one female slave but also meaning three milk cows.
54. I'll add as a note here that the word 'úath' is used a lot in this to describe the Morrigan and Cruachan in different ways - it's one of those fun words that has a lot of meanings from horrible, terrible, fear, specter, monster, phantom, hawthorn tree, cold, few, earth/clay...it's even the name of a type of story. I made a choice to stick with phantom pretty much throughout to give a sense of consistency equivalent to the repetition of the word in the Irish because I think to use different meanings would lose that feeling. However, one should keep in mind that where you see phantom it's a more layered nuance than just the English phantom and does have the overtones of frightening, etc.,
55. cor chuinnigh cairde might possibly also be read as "she seeks a heart friendship" or something similar. The words can mean both a legal respite or mercy, and should perhaps be understood as both.
56. The implication here is that because they fed her a meal, she owes them a forfeit, hence firu, "righteousness, truth" is given here as fulfillment although it could be read as well as "join with us against your righteousness"; the idea remains the same either way.
57. Brig can also be read as vigour, force, power, strength.
58. A name for Newgrange, roughly 'abode of [the] son of the youth' aka Oengus son of the Dagda and Boínn.

59. Sidhe – Otherworldly mound or hill.
60. Dur may also be read as firm, hard, severe or rigid.
61. Suirge may also mean lovemaking.
62. Tocbail can also be read as to raise up, bring up, or educate (as well as multiple other things)
63. i.e. a baby.
64. i.e. Oengus.
65. Duma treisc, literally 'mound of the trash' possibly a reference to the leavings of the feast
66. Ochan – a cry or groan of lament.
67. Derc may also be a pit or hole.
68. Currel is a word of uncertain meaning sometimes given as comb.
69. Literally reddening.
70. More literally was at that place in life, although bith can also be read as struck or wounded.
71. Literally battle rubbish or waste.
72. Matha – weak, soft, yielding.
73. Clannad can be a reference to setting up a gravestone.
74. Limbs, organs, any part of the body.
75. Con-berba, Cooked or boiled together.
76. A flat stone or rock.
77. Crag or peak of a mountain.
78. Front part or east.
79. Col can mean a range of things including sin, wrong, and violation.
80. Uncertain but possible 'one drink'.
81. Ustudh-builg, literally 'treasure-bag' but understood as craw or crop of an animal.
82. Staff or mace of fury or rage.
83. Note that rothraigh, a form of traigid, means both retreats as well as ebbs. Clearly meant as a play on words here.
84. I'm translating corn here as goblet but it can also be read as drinking horn. Certainly, drinking horn has a more poetic

feel with the names Curved-Horn and Eel, and the word tends to convey meanings attached to those shapes. I just went with goblet because it felt more regal in context.

85. Basically the word "cáech" means blind in one eye and this entry is a lot of linguistic gymnastics to explain Dian Cecht's name by explaining why it isn't related to blindness. In reality "cecht" is related to both learned knowledge, skill, ploughing, and later power (although this is probably a reflexive association coming from Dian Cecht's name).
86. Feocail is usually given here as "tooth" but it reads strangely to say that if the injury has no thorn in it then the person will lose a tooth, or teeth, for saying the charm. However, feocail is used poetically to mean a spike as well according to the eDIL and I find it more sensible to read it as I've translated it.
87. Mol – lump, rounded mass, heap.
88. Cruinniughadh – act of gathering collecting, hosting.
89. Goriath is uncertain and may also mean "piousness" giving us a cauldron of motion, a cauldron of piety, and a cauldron of honor (literally "face").
90. Ernbas, or iron-death is an idiom for death in battle by spear or sword point.
91. 'death on your mouth' and similar expressions are very common and can be find in many sources including the Táin Bó Fraích, and Cath Maige Mucruma.
92. The words used here that I'm translating at exploit and task are both forms of the same root word, bert, which can mean burden, covering, deed, exploit, task, trick or move in a game.
93. Emain Abhlach, emain of the apples, one of the si.

Bibliography

Best, R., (1916) 'Prognostications from the Raven and the Wren'; Ériu, vol. Retrieved from https://www.jstor.org/stable/30005405

Ebel, H., (1871) Grammatica Celtica.

Harleian MS 5280, fo 74a (n.d.) Retrieved from https://www.maryjones.us/ctexts/oengus_house.html

Herman, E., (1871) Grammatica Celtica. ed. Johann Kaspar

Hull, V., (1930) The Four jewels of the Tuatha Dé Danann. Zeitschrift für Celtische Philologie. vol 18

Irsan, Dublin, (n.d.) Trinity College, MS 1337 (H.3.18), Retrieved from http://www.asnc.cam.ac.uk/irishglossaries/

Lebar na Núachongbála, (n.d.)

Macalister, R., (1940). Lebor Gabala Erenn

MacNeill, E., and Murphy, G., (1908) Dunaire Finn. Retreived from https://archive.org/details/duanairefinnbook07macn

Meyer, K., (1903) Four Old-Irish Songs of Summer and Winter

Meyer, K., (1904) 'The Death of Conla [from the Yellow Book of Lecan, 214a], Eriu 1

Meyer, K., (1907) Archiv für Celtische Lexikographie

Meyer, K., (1908) 'Finn and the Man in the Tree'; Revue Celtique, vol 25

Meyer, K., (1910). Tochmarc Emire la Coinculaind

Meyer, K., (1911) Ancient Irish Poetry. Retrieved from https://www.maryjones.us/ctexts/vikings.html

O'Clery's Glossary, (n.d.) Retreieved from http://www.asnc.cam.ac.uk/irishglossaries/

O'Mulconry's Glossary, (n.d.) Retrieved from http://www.asnc.cam.ac.uk/irishglossaries/

Osbom, B., (1927). "How the Dagda Got His Magic Staff."

Sanas Cormaic, (n.d.) Retrieved from http://www.asnc.cam.ac.uk/irishglossaries/

Scéla Muicce Meic Dathó, (n.d.)
Shaw, F., (1934) Aislinge Óenguso
Stokes, W., & Windsch, E., (1880). Irische Texte mit Übersetzugen und Wörterbuch. Retreived from https://archive.org/details/irischetextemit00stokgoog/page/n10/mode/2up
Stokes, W., and Windsch, E., (1884) Irische Texte mit Übersetzugen und Wörterbuch. Retrieved from https://archive.org/details/irischetextemit01stokgoog/page/n7/mode/2up
Stokes, W., (1894). The Prose Tales of the Rennes Dindshenchas
Stokes, W., (1897). Cóir Anmann in Irische Texte mit Übersetzugen und Wörterbuch
Thurneyesen, R., (1896) 'Das Gedicht Der Vierzig Fragen Von Eochaid Ua Cerin' in Zeitschrift für celtische Philologie. Retrieved from https://archive.org/details/zeitschriftfrc13meyeuoft/page/130/mode/2up
Tonsing, E. (2012) "A Celtic Invocation: Cétnad nAíse," e-Keltoi: Journal of Interdisciplinary Celtic Studies: Vol. 8 Article 1.
Verba Scathaige, (nd) retrieved from https://storyarchaeology.com/wp-content/uploads/c21-Verba-Scathaige.pdf
Windisch, E., (1905) Tain Bo Cuiligne

About the Author

Morgan Daimler is a blogger, poet, teacher of esoteric subjects, witch, and priestess of the Daoine Maithe. Morgan is a prolific pagan writer, having published more than a dozen books under Moon Books alone, and she is one of the world's foremost experts on all things Fairy. Morgan lives in Connecticut, USA.

SELECTED TITLES

Irish Mythology
Lugh
The Dagda
The Morrigan
Irish Paganism
Raven Goddess
Manannán mac Lir

Norse Mythology
Odin
Thor
Freya
The Norse
Fairy Lore
Fairies
Fairycraft
Aos Sidhe
Fairy Witchcraft
21st Century Fairy
A New Dictionary of Fairies

MOON BOOKS

PAGANISM & SHAMANISM

What is Paganism? A religion, a spirituality, an alternative belief system, nature worship? You can find support for all these definitions (and many more) in dictionaries, encyclopaedias, and text books of religion, but subscribe to any one and the truth will evade you. Above all Paganism is a creative pursuit, an encounter with reality, an exploration of meaning and an expression of the soul. Druids, Heathens, Wiccans, and others, all contribute their insights and literary riches to the Pagan tradition. Moon Books invites you to begin or to deepen your own encounter, right here, right now.

If you have enjoyed this book, why not tell other readers by posting a review on your preferred book site.

Bestsellers from Moon Books

Pagan Portals Series

The Morrigan

Meeting the Great Queens

Morgan Daimler

Ancient and enigmatic, the Morrigan reaches out to us. On shadowed wings and in raven's call, meet the ancient Irish goddess of war, battle, prophecy, death, sovereignty, and magic.

Paperback: 978-1-78279-833-0 ebook: 978-1-78279-834-7

The Awen Alone

Walking the Path of the Solitary Druid

Joanna van der Hoeven

An introductory guide for the solitary Druid, The Awen Alone will accompany you as you explore, and seek out your own place within the natural world.

Paperback: 978-1-78279-547-6 ebook: 978-1-78279-546-9

Moon Magic

Rachel Patterson

An introduction to working with the phases of the Moon, what they are and how to live in harmony with the lunar year and to utilise all the magical powers it provides.

Paperback: 978-1-78279-281-9 ebook: 978-1-78279-282-6

Hekate

A Devotional

Vivienne Moss

Hekate, Queen of Witches and the Shadow-Lands, haunts the pages of this devotional bringing magic and enchantment into your lives.

Paperback: 978-1-78535-161-7 ebook: 978-1-78535-162-4

Bestsellers from Moon Books

Keeping Her Keys

An Introduction to Hekate's Modern Witchcraft

Cyndi Brannen

Blending Hekate, witchcraft and personal development together to create a powerful new magickal perspective.

Paperback: 978-1-78904-075-3 ebook 978-1-78904-076-0

Journey to the Dark Goddess

How to Return to Your Soul

Jane Meredith

Discover the powerful secrets of the Dark Goddess and transform your depression, grief and pain into healing and integration.

Paperback: 978-1-84694-677-6 ebook: 978-1-78099-223-5

Shamanic Reiki

Expanded Ways of Working with Universal Life Force Energy

Llyn Roberts, Robert Levy

Shamanism and Reiki are each powerful ways of healing; together, their power multiplies. Shamanic Reiki introduces techniques to help healers and Reiki practitioners tap ancient healing wisdom.

Paperback: 978-1-84694-037-8 ebook: 978-1-84694-650-9

Southern Cunning

Folkloric Witchcraft in the American South

Aaron Oberon

Modern witchcraft with a Southern flair, this book is a journey through the folklore of the American South and a look at the power these stories hold for modern witches.

Paperback: 978-1-78904-196-5 ebook: 978-1-78904-197-2

Readers of ebooks can buy or view any of these bestsellers by clicking on the live link in the title. Most titles are published in paperback and as an ebook. Paperbacks are available in traditional bookshops. Both print and ebook formats are available online.

Find more titles and sign up to our readers' newsletter
http://www.johnhuntpublishing.com/paganism

YouTube

For video content, author interviews and more, please subscribe to our YouTube channel.

MoonBooksPublishing

Follow us on social media for book news, promotions and more:

Facebook: Moon Books

Instagram: @MoonBooksCI

X: @MoonBooksCI

TikTok: @MoonBooksCI